Decoding Bible Messages

JOHN A. MAPP JR.

To Jenna and Troy,

May God make all of your dreams and heart-desires come true. This book certainly fulfills one of mine.

In Christ,

John A. Mapp, Jr

WESTBOW PRESS®
A DIVISION OF THOMAS NELSON
& ZONDERVAN

Copyright © 2015 John A. Mapp Jr.

All rights reserved. No part of this book may be used or reproduced by any means, graphic, electronic, or mechanical, including photocopying, recording, taping or by any information storage retrieval system without the written permission of the author except in the case of brief quotations embodied in critical articles and reviews.

This book is a work of non-fiction. Unless otherwise noted, the author and the publisher make no explicit guarantees as to the accuracy of the information contained in this book and in some cases, names of people and places have been altered to protect their privacy.

WestBow Press books may be ordered through booksellers or by contacting:

WestBow Press
A Division of Thomas Nelson & Zondervan
1663 Liberty Drive
Bloomington, IN 47403
www.westbowpress.com
1 (866) 928-1240

Because of the dynamic nature of the Internet, any web addresses or links contained in this book may have changed since publication and may no longer be valid. The views expressed in this work are solely those of the author and do not necessarily reflect the views of the publisher, and the publisher hereby disclaims any responsibility for them.

Any people depicted in stock imagery provided by Thinkstock are models, and such images are being used for illustrative purposes only.
Certain stock imagery © Thinkstock.

Unless otherwise identified, Scripture quotations in this publication are taken from *The Holy Bible, New International Version®, NIV®*. Copyright © 1973, 1978, 1984, 2011 by Biblica, Inc.® Used by permission. All rights reserved worldwide.

Scripture quotations marked "TLB" are taken from *The Living Bible,* copyright © 1971 by Tyndale House Foundation. Used by permission of Tyndale House Publishers Inc., Carol Stream, Illinois 60188. All rights reserved.

Scripture quotations marked "NKJV" are taken from the New King James Version®. Copyright © 1982 by Thomas Nelson. Used by permission. All rights reserved.

Scripture quotations marked "KJV" are taken from the King James Version.

ISBN: 978-1-5127-1039-7 (sc)
ISBN: 978-1-5127-1040-3 (hc)
ISBN: 978-1-5127-1038-0 (e)

Library of Congress Control Number: 2015914044

Print information available on the last page.

WestBow Press rev. date: 9/15/2015

CONTENTS

Introduction vii
1   New Life in Old Bible Stories 1
2   Decoding the Account of Adam and Eve 7
3   Decoding the First Garments 13
4   Decoding the Garden of Eden 17
5   Decoding the Flood and Noah's Ark 25
6   Decoding the Life of Isaac 31
7   Decoding the Life of Joseph 37
8   Decoding the Life of Moses 45
9   Decoding the First Passover and the Exodus 53
10 Decoding the Wilderness Years: Part 1 59
11 Decoding the Wilderness Years: Part 2 67
12 Decoding the Tabernacle and the Temple 73
13 Decoding the Gospel of John 81
14 Decoding the Life of David 87
15 Decoding the Lives of the Heroes of the Faith 93
16 Decoding the Recurring Symbols of the Bible 99
17 Decoding the Signs of God's Presence 105
18 Decoding the Names of God 111
19 Decoding the Birth Pangs of Israel 115
20 The Holographic Testament 123
Bibliography 127

INTRODUCTION

Jesus of Nazareth is the pivotal figure in human history. The entire Bible, from Genesis to Revelation, is about Him. There are many notable Old Testament passages that forecast details of His life with amazing accuracy. Some of these passages, such as the Isaiah 53 account of the suffering servant, refer directly to Jesus and are well known to many Christians. Other passages, however, appear to have nothing at all to do with Jesus at first glance because they are couched in symbolism and must be "decoded."

For example, the book of Exodus sets forth the following instructions regarding the handling and eating of the Passover lamb: "It must be eaten inside the house. Take none of the meat outside the house. Do not break any of the bones" (Exodus 12:46). There were no indications given at the time that the instructions needed to be taken at any more than their face value.

But many years later, when John described the crucifixion of Jesus in his gospel, he noted that the Roman soldiers did not break Jesus's legs as He hung on the cross (which was the usual practice during a crucifixion), but instead they thrust a spear into His side. This happened, John explained, "so that the scripture would be fulfilled: 'Not one of his bones will be broken'" (John 19:36). At this point, we see that God had more in mind than merely establishing the Passover ceremony when He presented Moses and Aaron with regulations for the Passover meal. This and many other Old Testament passages, along with the events they describe, symbolically foreshadowed the life and death of the Jewish Messiah.

This book's goal is to illuminate some of these passages and events, and to show the reader how to study the Bible, particularly the Old Testament, with new insight. The result will be a heightened appreciation of the inspired nature of the Bible and of God's care and concern for His people throughout history.

CHAPTER 1
New Life in Old Bible Stories

A long time ago in the land of Israel, an innocent man in the prime of life was led up the side of a hill to die a sacrificial death. He had led an interesting life. The circumstances surrounding his birth were especially unusual. He was miraculously conceived, and his parents had been visited by an angel who foretold the event. The Lord even provided the surprised parents-to-be with a name for the child.

Now, as he strained under his wooden burden, this man trusted completely in his father and subjected himself to his father's will. He was to be laid upon the wood, pierced, and slain as a sacrifice.

But it was not yet Isaac's time to die. An angel stepped in at the last moment and stayed Abraham's hand. This event must have perplexed Isaac. But little did he realize the remarkable way in which the defining moments of his life resembled defining moments in the life of the Messiah, who was to come some two thousand years later.

The events recounted above are taken from Genesis, chapters 17, 18, and 22. However, their resemblance to the gospel accounts of Jesus's life is striking. It seems God had much more in mind than testing Abraham's faith. By working through the events in Isaac's life, God presented His redemptive nature in a prophetic portrait of Jesus Christ.

This kind of prophetic portrait, not quite an explicit

prophecy but more than a mere historical account, is commonly referred to as a "type." In essence, a type is anything in the Old Testament that symbolically foreshadows a thing, event, or character in the New Testament. The term originated in the Bible itself, in Paul's first letter to the Corinthians: "Now all these things happened unto them for ensamples: and they are written for our admonition, upon whom the ends of the world are come" (1 Corinthians 10:11 KJV).

Many Bible versions have a marginal note stating that the word *ensamples,* or *examples,* comes from a Greek word meaning "types." This is the term most Bible commentators use when referring to these hidden pictures in the Old Testament.

First Corinthians goes on to provide a New Testament understanding of several of the most well-known experiences encountered by the Israelites during their time in the wilderness. These include the parted waters of the Red Sea, the cloud that led the Israelites about, the rock that yielded water, the manna that sustained the wanderers, and even the character of Moses. The experiences with the sea and the cloud are compared with a baptism, and the rock is identified with Christ, the provider of living water.

A type differs from a prophecy in important ways. As an example of a prophecy, consider this passage from the prophet Isaiah: "He was oppressed and afflicted, yet he did not open his mouth; he was led like a lamb to the slaughter, and as a sheep before her shearers is silent, so he did not open his mouth" (Isaiah 53:7). This passage clearly describes how the Messiah would stand before His accusers in silence, like a lamb. The prophecy was fulfilled when Jesus maintained silence before Pontius Pilate.

The book of Exodus, as noted in the introduction, provides God's instructions on the handling of the first Passover lamb. The Lord told Moses and Aaron, "Do not break any of the bones" (Exodus 12:46). Only in light of the New Testament do we realize that these instructions foreshadowed the manner in which Jesus would die.

Prophecies, therefore, tend to be explicit forecasts of future events. Types, however, are found in Bible passages describing historical people and events, with no obvious reference to the future. But on closer examination, we often find many symbolic references to subsequent events buried in these passages.

In 1 Corinthians 10:6–12, the Bible commends the study of types to help keep us from repeating some of the mistakes of the past. The types also help us understand the importance of Christ's death and resurrection. In fact, so important are some of the types that the Lord had His New Testament writers explain them clearly in the Scriptures. For example, in explaining the structure and functions of the temple, the book of Hebrews says,

> But only the high priest entered the inner room, and that only once a year, and never without blood, which he offered for himself and for the sins the people had committed in ignorance. The Holy Spirit was showing by this that the way into the Most Holy Place had not yet been disclosed as long as the first tabernacle was still functioning. This is an illustration for the present time, indicating that the gifts and sacrifices being offered were not able to clear the conscience of the worshiper. (Hebrews 9:7–9)

But when Christ died on the cross, "The curtain of the temple was torn in two from top to bottom" (Mark 15:38). The book of Hebrews concludes,

> And so, dear brothers, now we may walk right into the very Holy of Holies where God is,

> because of the blood of Jesus. This is the fresh, new, life-giving way which Christ has opened up for us by tearing the curtain—his human body—to let us into the holy presence of God. (Hebrews 10:19–20 TLB)

The book of Hebrews explains that the curtain of the temple that separated the Holy of Holies from the adjacent chamber was a type of Christ's human body. The tearing of the curtain represented the tearing of Christ's body on the cross. The way to the Father was made available to us through this death on the cross.

It is also noteworthy that the curtain of the temple was torn from top to bottom. This was clearly an act of God and not of humans. In like manner, Jesus's sacrifice was God's initiative and not humankind's.

There is strong scriptural evidence to suggest that Jesus personally thought very highly of the types and taught them to His disciples. While walking on the road to Emmaus with two of His disciples, the newly resurrected Jesus found it necessary to provide a detailed review of the Old Testament to overcome their slowness of comprehension.

> "Did not the Messiah have to suffer these things and then enter his glory?" And beginning with Moses and all the Prophets, he explained to them what was said in all the Scriptures concerning himself. (Luke 24:26–27)

The disciples' hearts burned within them as they heard the Scriptures explained in new ways. Yet it is common knowledge that the Jews of the time were very familiar with their own Scriptures. So the disciples must have already known about most of the messianic prophecies in the Old Testament. Jesus may have explained some of them in a new light while walking with His disciples. But He was probably also explaining some of the types to them for the first time. It wasn't until His crucifixion and resurrection that many of these types became explainable.

The book of Luke describes another of Jesus's postresurrection teaching sessions.

> He said to them, "This is what I told you while I was still with you: Everything must be fulfilled that is written about me in the Law of Moses, the Prophets and the Psalms." Then he opened their minds so they could understand the Scriptures. He told them, "This is what is written: The Messiah will suffer and rise from the dead on the third day, and repentance for the forgiveness of sins will be preached in his name to all nations, beginning at Jerusalem." (Luke 24:44–47)

Note that Jesus said, "The Law of Moses, the Prophets and the Psalms." That covers almost all of what we know today as the Old Testament. These writings, Jesus said, contain passages "written about me." Here we see a very important key to understanding the Bible. Not only the New Testament but also the entire Bible, from Genesis to Revelation, is about Jesus Christ. Jesus was not an afterthought on His Father's part; instead, He was the ultimate object of all of God's dealings with humanity related in the Old Testament. The types of the Old Testament, when considered in addition to the prophecies, doubly reinforce this point. When the Bible reader grasps this, the entire Bible comes alive with new meaning.

An understanding of types is necessary if one is to comprehend many New Testament passages. For example, Jesus made a curious statement to Nathaniel after they first met: "Very truly I tell you, you will see 'heaven open, and the angels of God ascending and descending on' the Son of Man" (John 1:51).

What did He mean by this? The key to understanding this passage is contained in an experience Jacob had almost two thousand years earlier as he was camping in the wilderness: "He had a dream in which he saw a stairway resting on the earth, with its top reaching to heaven, and the angels of God were ascending and descending on it" (Genesis 28:12).

It is evident from this passage that Jesus was referring to Jacob's ladder. The celebrated ladder Jacob saw in his dream was a type of Jesus Christ. Jesus Himself decoded Jacob's old dream. Just as the ladder stretched from heaven to earth, so does Jesus form a bridge, of sorts, between heaven and earth—our one Way to heaven. Jesus said, "I am the way and the truth and the life. No one comes to the Father except through me" (John 14:6).

An understanding of the types cannot help but increase our appreciation of the inspired nature of the Bible. Some of these types forecast parts of Jesus's life down to the minutest details. It is simply not adequate to think of the Old Testament merely as a series of history lessons about Israel. It is a book about Jesus, even though it was written hundreds of years before He was a gleam in His mother's eye.

Finally, the types demonstrate the sovereignty of God. They show us beyond doubt that God was actively at work in the life of Israel, carefully governing the events that took place, weaving into them numerous prophetic pictures of the coming Messiah. We can take heart from this and know that God is continually working His purpose in our own lives, even during our darkest hours.

To summarize, the study of the types benefits us in several ways. We learn not to repeat the mistakes of the Israelites. We arrive at a better understanding of many specific Bible passages. Our appreciation of the inspired nature of the whole Bible is enhanced, as is our appreciation of God's love and sovereignty.

CHAPTER 2
Decoding the Account of Adam and Eve

Much attention has been focused on the passage in Ephesians that directs a wife to submit herself to her husband's leadership. Often overlooked is the much greater reciprocal obligation of the husband: to love his wife in such an unconditional and self-sacrificing way that his love resembles the love of Jesus Christ for His church:

> Husbands ought to love their wives as their own bodies. He who loves his wife loves himself. After all, no one ever hated their own body, but they feed and care for their body, just as Christ does the church—for we are members of his body. "For this reason a man will leave his father and mother and be united to his wife, and the two will become one flesh." This is a profound mystery—but I am talking about Christ and the church. (Ephesians 5:28–32)

This passage of Scripture tells us that a healthy relationship between a husband and wife may be compared to the relationship between Christ and the church. The book of Revelation even refers to the church as the bride of Christ. It should therefore come as no surprise to find a portrait of Christ and the church hidden in the account of the very first marriage.

Note, first of all, that the passage of Scripture just quoted contains a direct quotation from the Genesis account of Adam and Eve. It should therefore be instructive to take a closer look at the passage in Genesis from which the quote was taken:

> So the Lord God caused the man to fall into a deep sleep; and while he was sleeping, he took one of the man's ribs and closed up the place with flesh. Then the Lord God made a woman from the rib he had taken out of the man, and he brought her to the man. The man said, "This is now bone of my bones and flesh of my flesh; she shall be called 'woman,' for she was taken out of man." That is why a man leaves his father and mother and is united to his wife, and they become one flesh. (Genesis 2:21–24)

In order for Eve to be formed, a deep sleep had to fall upon Adam and his flesh had to be wounded. Likewise, in order for the church to be formed, a deep sleep had to fall upon a severely wounded Christ as He died and spent three days in the grave. After the work was complete, Adam was revived from his sleep just as Jesus was raised from the dead. Since Eve was made from one of Adam's ribs, she could consider herself a member of Adam's body. In like manner, the Bible teaches that Christians are members of the body of Christ. Genesis 2:24 states, "A man leaves his father and mother and is united to his wife, and they become one flesh." Jesus left the home He had with His Father in heaven to be born into the world in order to become the husband of His church. By partaking of the body and blood of Christ during Communion, we affirm today that we have become one flesh with Him.

When a marriage takes place, not only does the husband

leave his home and his parents, but also the bride must leave her home. And so it is with Christians. We must forsake the things of this world and embrace the kingdom of God as our new home, even while still dwelling physically on earth.

God created Eve so that Adam would have a helper and a companion. Once we become Christians, we are called to be Christ's helpers, doing "good works, which God prepared in advance for us to do" (Ephesians 2:10).

We see from these comparisons that the relationship between Adam and Eve is a beautiful type of the relationship between Jesus Christ and His church.

But there are other ways in which Adam resembles Christ. It is from Adam that the entire human race is descended. Jesus too is the head of a race of people: He is the firstborn of many believers who are to form one family through faith in Him. When God created the world, He said it was "very good" (Genesis 1:31). When Jesus was baptized, "A voice from heaven said, 'This is my Son, whom I love; with him I am well pleased'" (Matthew 3:17). So there was a heavenly expression of approval for both Adam and Jesus: when Adam was created and when Jesus was baptized.

In each case, the Devil appeared on the scene immediately after with a temptation to offer. In the first case, the Devil prevailed since Adam succumbed to the temptation to eat of the forbidden fruit. But in the second case, Christ did not succumb to the temptation. He refused to use His power to turn stones into bread.

It is interesting to note that both of these temptations had to do with food. The Devil approached Adam at a time when Adam was in a position of great strength. He had just been created by God, who gave him power over the earth. In addition, God had instructed him in his responsibilities and had even provided him with a helper. Adam was almost literally on top of the world. He was immortal, united with God, and had perfect communion with Him. He had access to all the food he needed on the trees around him. And yet, despite having just one simple rule to obey, he broke it.

Jesus, on the other hand, was at His weakest when the Devil approached Him. He had just spent forty days and nights fasting in the wilderness. He must have been extremely hungry. The Devil, characteristically, hit Him at His weakest point: "If you are the Son of God, tell these stones to become bread," he said (Matthew 4:3). But Jesus knew it was not His Father's will for Him to take the easy way out and to break the discipline of the fast, and so He refused even though it was well within His power to perform the miracle Satan had suggested. Thus, while Adam had failed an easy test, Jesus passed a most grueling and arduous test. In the process, He administered a stinging defeat to Satan.

As the case of the two temptations implies, it is through the contrasts that we see the most illuminating parallels between these two lives. The Scriptures themselves go a long way toward illustrating these contrasts. The book of 1 Corinthians contrasts the work of Adam with the work of Christ: from Adam there arose a natural, perishable body sown in dishonor and weakness, whereas from Christ there arose a spiritual, imperishable body raised in glory and power. The passage goes on:

> If there is a natural body, there is also a spiritual body. So it is written: "The first man Adam became a living being"; the last Adam, a life-giving spirit. The spiritual did not come first, but the natural, and after that the spiritual. The first man was of the dust of the earth; the second man is of heaven. (1 Corinthians 15:44–47)

The book of Romans expands upon the contrasts between Adam and Christ:

> For if, by the trespass of the one man, death reigned through that one man, how much more will those who receive God's abundant provision of grace and of the gift of righteousness reign in life through the one man, Jesus Christ! Consequently, just as one trespass resulted in condemnation for all people, so also one righteous act resulted in justification and life for all people. For just as through the disobedience of the one man the many were made sinners, so also through the obedience of the one man the many will be made righteous. (Romans 5:17–19)

Jesus effectively reversed the work of Adam and even lived Adam's life in reverse. Consider the diagram in figure 1. In the beginning, when Adam was created, he was united with God and was immortal. He was given dominion over the earth. Then Adam acquired sin through his disobedience. This resulted in his expulsion from the garden of Eden. In addition, he became mortal and eventually died. The result was that the whole human race was separated from God and in a very desperate situation. Christ reversed the damage Adam had done. But He had to pick up the loose ends where Adam had left them. Jesus was born into the world as a man; He was beaten, humiliated, and crucified; and He took all of our sins upon Himself. God then raised Him from the dead and gave all power on heaven and earth to Him. Christ will return in great power and glory at some future time, and all things will be put under Him. The final result is that death will be overcome. We will be reunited with God and will be immortal, just as Adam was intended to be.

So there is a remarkable symmetry between the life of Adam and the life of Jesus Christ, making Adam a striking type of Christ, although more through contrasts than through similarities.

FIGURE 1

CHRIST: THE LAST ADAM

ADAM:

A. MAN CREATED. UNITED WITH GOD. IMMORTAL.

LIVING BEING

B. ADAM GIVEN DOMINION OVER THE WORLD.

C. ACQUIRED SIN AND DIED SPIRITUALLY.

D. DISGRACED: EXPELLED FROM EDEN.

E. BECAME A MORTAL AND DIED.

RESULT: MAN SEPARATED FROM GOD.

E'. CHRIST BORN A MAN.

CHRIST:

D'. DISGRACED: BEATEN AND HUMILIATED.

C'. DIED CARRYING ALL OF OUR SINS.

LIFE-GIVING SPIRIT

B'. RAISED AND GIVEN DOMINION OVER THE WORLD.

A'. MAN REUNITED WITH GOD. DEATH OVERCOME.

CHAPTER 3
Decoding the First Garments

The Devil employed some of his standard tricks when he enticed Eve into eating the forbidden fruit: He appealed to her pride and envy, telling her, "Your eyes will be opened, and you will be like God, knowing good and evil" (Genesis 3:5). He also got her to doubt the Word of God by putting a question in her mind ("Did God really say...?" [Genesis 3:1]). One reason these tactics succeeded is that Adam, it would appear, had done a poor job of passing along God's instructions to Eve. She thought God had commanded them not to touch the forbidden fruit (Genesis 3:3), when in fact there is no indication that God had said anything about touching it. Perhaps this was because Adam was overprotective. In any case, the result was that Satan was able to persuade Eve that it was all right to eat the fruit. Adam also ate the fruit, even though he knew better. Why Adam followed his wife's lead may never be known for sure this side of eternity. Perhaps he was so in love with his wife that he would have done anything to avoid being separated from her. After all, theirs was a marriage that was literally made in heaven. Jesus likewise went to the cross to avoid being separated from us, but the comparison breaks down at this point because Jesus, unlike Adam, committed no sin.

After Adam and Eve had both eaten the fruit, "The eyes of both of them were opened, and they realized they were naked; so they sewed fig leaves together and made coverings for themselves" (Genesis 3:7). Then they hid from God in fear.

Immediately after the fall of Adam and Eve and their alienation from God, the Lord began to help them pick up the pieces of their shattered lives. The first thing God did was seek them out and confront them, just as a concerned father would do. He took away their immortality and expelled them from the garden of Eden. But before the expulsion, He promised that one of Eve's male descendants would crush the head of the Serpent, signifying the defeat of Satan (Genesis 3:15). Then God "made garments of skin for Adam and his wife and clothed them" (Genesis 3:21).

Note that God replaced their garments of fig leaves with garments of animal skins. It appears that this was God's way of introducing humanity to the practice of sacrificing animals. We now know that the animal sacrifices of the Old Testament symbolized the death of Jesus on the cross at Calvary. So the animal skins with which God clothed Adam and Eve spoke of the death of Jesus because animals had to be sacrificed to make these garments. In a similar way, Jesus had to be sacrificed on the cross and then be raised from the dead to enable us to be clothed with the righteousness of Christ and to put on the armor of God.

Now consider the garments of fig leaves. By the very nature of the fabrication process, the leaves had to be separated from the fig plants. Separated from the vine, the leaves would quickly die. As Jesus told His disciples,

> No branch can bear fruit by itself; it must remain in the vine. Neither can you bear fruit unless you remain in me. I am the vine; you are the branches. If you remain in me and I in you, you will bear much fruit; apart from me you can do nothing. (John 15:4–5)

Decoding Bible Messages

The account of the two kinds of garments illustrates perfectly the difference between our way and God's way. The best clothing solution that Adam and Eve could devise was garments of fig leaves. These garments were highly temporary, becoming dried and withered soon after they were made. The symbolism of these garments actually reinforces the idea of humanity's separation from God. Our way may look appealing, and it may seem logical at the time, but even our best is not good enough. God Himself provided the enduring garments Adam and Eve really needed, while at the same time foreshadowing the sacrifice of Jesus Christ and the clothing of the believers with Christ's righteousness through His shed blood.

From this episode we may also gain some insight into the offerings of Cain and Abel. In the account in the book of Genesis, we see the facts concerning these two offerings:

> Now Abel kept flocks, and Cain worked the soil. In the course of time Cain brought some of the fruits of the soil as an offering to the Lord. And Abel also brought an offering—fat portions from some of the firstborn of his flock. The Lord looked with favor on Abel and his offering, but on Cain and his offering he did not look with favor. So Cain was very angry, and his face was downcast. (Genesis 4:2–5)

We are not explicitly told why God was displeased with Cain's offering. Perhaps it was Cain's bad attitude. Or perhaps he only brought God the leftovers. But perhaps, too, the offering did not meet God's criteria for portraying the coming Messiah. There would not seem to be any messianic symbolism in Cain's offering.

However, Abel's offering clearly spoke of the coming

Messiah. It was an animal sacrifice, following the pattern set by God when He made the first lasting garments worn by Adam and Eve. The offering also came from the firstborn of Abel's flock, just as Jesus was "the firstborn over all creation" and "the firstborn from among the dead" (Colossians 1:15, 18). So Abel's offering was accepted by God.

People who put God first often incur the disapproval of others, and so it was with Abel. Cain, furious with envy, slew his brother in anger. However, Abel was remembered for his faith and righteousness (Hebrews 11:4), and his name will surely be found in the Lamb's Book of Life.

CHAPTER 4
Decoding the Garden of Eden

The first chapter of the book of Genesis tells how God brought order out of chaos. He separated light from darkness and seas from dry land. He formed the heavenly bodies and gave order to their movements. He created the sun to light the earth by day, and the moon to light the earth by night.

When God finished creating the world, it was a perfect work. It was a world devoid of violence, destruction, and death. Adam was sinless and united with God by a close personal relationship, and God had placed him in charge of the garden of Eden. Food was readily available on the trees and the other plants that covered the earth. In keeping with the peace and abundance of this world, the animals were all vegetarians, as were the people (Genesis 1:29–30).

Although the world was perfect when Adam and Eve were created, we know that God's creation was not totally unaffected by evil, for Satan had already fallen by the time the first humans arrived on the scene. Our first glimpse of Satan shows him crawling around upon the earth, inhabiting the body of a serpent and successfully enticing Eve to eat the forbidden fruit.

After Adam and Eve succumbed to the Serpent's evil temptation, the Lord confronted all three of them. He did not act in haste. He even gave Adam and Eve a chance to explain themselves. However, finding their explanations inadequate, He proceeded to pronounce five curses upon His creation.

The first curse was upon the Serpent:

> So the Lord God said to the serpent, "Because you have done this, cursed are you above all livestock and all wild animals! You will crawl on your belly and you will eat dust all the days of your life." (Genesis 3:14)

Thus, the serpent became the loathsome, legless creature it is today. Note also, however, that this curse included the entire animal kingdom, for if the serpent was cursed "above all livestock and all wild animals," then the animals themselves must have been cursed too, though to a lesser degree. Thus, some animals became predators. No longer would the lion lie down with the lamb, except to feast on its dead carcass.

The next verse seems to be a continuation of the curse upon the Serpent, but there is more to it than that: "And I will put enmity between you and the woman, and between your offspring and hers; he will crush your head, and you will strike his heel" (Genesis 3:15).

On one level, this seems to be saying that people and snakes would henceforth have a hard time getting along with one another. This has certainly proven true over the years. But on another level, it is a prophecy of the coming Messiah, the first such prophecy in the Bible. Note that the Bible refers to the offspring of the woman as a "he," meaning a particular male descendant. The serpent, of course, represents Satan, who inhabited the snake's body. The Scripture says that this male descendant of Eve will crush the head of Satan but will have his heel struck in the process. In light of the New Testament, we now know that Jesus of Nazareth is the promised male descendant of Eve who will destroy Satan. Note also that He is referred to as the offspring of the *woman*, not

Decoding Bible Messages

as the offspring of the man and the woman. This is because His human parentage included only His mother Mary, for He was conceived by the Holy Spirit. The striking of His heel must refer to His crucifixion. How much worse, then, must Satan's fate be if it is symbolized by the crushing of his head!

God's next curse was upon Eve: "I will make your pains in childbearing very severe; with painful labor you will give birth to children. Your desire will be for your husband, and he will rule over you" (Genesis 3:16).

There followed a long period in human history, one persisting in many cultures up to this day, in which women were subservient to men.

The Lord then, speaking to Adam, pronounced a curse upon the ground:

> Because you listened to your wife and ate fruit from the tree about which I commanded you, "You must not eat from it," Cursed is the ground because of you; through painful toil you will eat food from it all the days of your life. It will produce thorns and thistles for you, and you will eat the plants of the field.
> (Genesis 3:17–18)

Food would no longer be available in abundance without hard work. Agriculture became the principal occupation of humankind for the next several thousand years.

God's final curse was upon Adam himself: "By the sweat of your brow you will eat your food until you return to the ground, since from it you were taken; for dust you are and to dust you will return" (Genesis 3:19). Thus, the Lord established for human beings a life that would be both difficult and short.

The Lord then drove Adam and Eve from the garden of Eden and, in the process, took steps to ensure that human beings would not have access to the Tree of Life. Even in the midst of this severe punishment, however, we see that the Lord still loved us and had our best interests at heart, for if man (in the generic sense) were "allowed to reach out his hand and take also from the tree of life and eat, and live forever" (Genesis 3:22), he would have lived forever in his fallen condition and could never have been redeemed by any means we know of, for the death of Jesus could not have occurred. Thus, the Lord immediately began laying the groundwork for our salvation even as He was meting out our punishment.

The last three chapters of the book of Revelation describe the final fulfillment of that salvation. It is very instructive to examine these chapters, for we see in them the completion of everything that was set into motion in the first three chapters of the book of Genesis. There are some stunning similarities between these two passages of Scripture.

The book of Revelation makes it clear that the Lord will amply compensate us for "the years the locusts have eaten" (Joel 2:25). In fact, the final state of humanity will be even better than the first.

The final roadblock to this restoration will be eliminated when "that ancient serpent" Satan (Revelation 20:2) receives the punishment promised to him in the book of Genesis. We have seen Satan's first deception described in Genesis. We see Satan's final deception described in Revelation:

> When the thousand years are over, Satan will be released from his prison and will go out to deceive the nations in the four corners of the earth—Gog and Magog—and to gather them for battle. In number they are like the sand on the seashore. They marched across the breadth of the earth and surrounded the camp of God's people, the city he loves. But

fire came down from heaven and devoured them. (Revelation 20:7–9)

Likewise, we see in the book of Revelation the fulfillment of the doom promised to Satan in Genesis 3:15:

> And the devil, who deceived them, was thrown into the lake of burning sulfur, where the beast and the false prophet had been thrown. They will be tormented day and night for ever and ever. (Revelation 20:10)

The apostle John also writes:

> Then I saw "a new heaven and a new earth," for the first heaven and the first earth had passed away, and there was no longer any sea. I saw the Holy City, the new Jerusalem, coming down out of heaven from God, prepared as a bride beautifully dressed for her husband. (Revelation 21:1–2)

Thus, while there had been seas in the original creation, there will be no more seas in the new earth. Humanity's first home was in a garden. Humanity's eternal home will be in a beautiful city. There will also be other noteworthy changes:

- The city does not need the sun or the moon to shine on it, for the glory of God gives it light, and the Lamb is its lamp. (Revelation 21:23)

- There will be no more night. They will not need the light of a lamp or the light of the sun, for the Lord God will give them light. (Revelation 22:5)

And so we see there will be no more night there, and no need for the sun or the moon. We will once more enjoy the quality of life and the close fellowship with God that our first ancestors had in the garden of Eden:

- He will wipe every tear from their eyes. There will be no more death or mourning or crying or pain, for the old order of things has passed away. (Revelation 21:4)

- No longer will there be any curse. The throne of God and of the Lamb will be in the city, and his servants will serve him. They will see his face, and his name will be on their foreheads. (Revelation 22:3–4)

Whereas the first earth had been ruled by the first Adam, the new earth will be ruled by the last Adam, the Lord Jesus Christ.

Finally, we will once more have access to the Tree of Life from which we had been banished: "Blessed are those who wash their robes, that they may have the right to the tree of life and may go through the gates into the city" (Revelation 22:14).

Figure 2 shows the symmetrical relationship between the books of Genesis and Revelation, indicating how all of the damage done by Original Sin is repaired, bringing us full circle to a state of Eden-like paradise. It is clear from these comparisons that the garden of Eden is a type of the New Jerusalem, God's everlasting home for His people.

It is also clear that God's Word is remarkably consistent from start to finish. We may rest assured that all He has said will come to pass. Though the books of the Bible have many different human authors, they are all inspired by God. How else could two books written by two different people some fifteen hundred years apart be combined to portray such elegant symmetry in God's plan for the world?

FIGURE 2

FROM GENESIS TO REVELATION: A FULL CIRCLE

GENESIS		REVELATION	
GEN. 1:2-5	DARKNESS	REV. 22:5	NO NIGHT THERE
GEN. 1:10	SEAS	REV. 21:1	NO MORE SEA
GEN. 1:16-17	MADE THE SUN AND MOON	REV. 21:23	NO NEED OF SUN OR MOON
GEN. 2:8	MAN'S FIRST HOME A GARDEN	REV. 21:2	MAN'S ETERNAL HOME A CITY
GEN. 2:15	THE FIRST EARTH RULED BY ADAM	REV. 22:3-4	THE NEW EARTH RULED BY JESUS
GEN. 3:16-19	ENTRANCE OF DEATH, SORROW, AND PAIN	REV. 21:4	NO MORE DEATH, SORROW, OR PAIN
GEN. 3:17	CURSE	REV. 22:3	NO MORE CURSE
GEN. 3:22-24	BANISHMENT FROM THE GARDEN, AND FROM THE TREE OF LIFE	REV. 22:2, 13-14	RESTORED ACCESS TO THE TREE OF LIFE IN THE NEW JERUSALEM
GEN. 3:1-6	SATAN'S FIRST DECEPTION	REV. 20:7-9	SATAN'S LAST DECEPTION
GEN. 3:14-15	SATAN'S DOOM FORETOLD	REV. 20:2, 10	SATAN ("THAT OLD SERPENT") BOUND, THEN DESTROYED

CHAPTER 5
Decoding the Flood and Noah's Ark

The Lord had to take some extraordinary steps to preserve and prepare humanity for the coming of the deliverer promised in Genesis 3:15.

We are told in 1 Peter 1:12 that "even angels long to look into" the things pertaining to our salvation. As the heavenly host watched the drama unfolding on the earth below, the angels must have wondered how God would bring about the fulfillment of His promise to send a Savior who would crush the head of the Serpent. At times, things must have looked completely hopeless to the angelic observers. As Adam and Eve's descendants multiplied, they began to turn away from God, increasingly turning toward wickedness. The result of this grim trend is described in the sixth chapter of Genesis:

> When human beings began to increase in number on the earth and daughters were born to them, the sons of God saw that the daughters of humans were beautiful, and they married any of them they chose. ... The Nephilim were on the earth in those days—and also afterward—when the sons of God went to the daughters of humans and had children by them. They were the heroes of old, men of renown. The Lord saw how great the wickedness of the human

> race had become on the earth, and that every inclination of the thoughts of the human heart was only evil all the time. (Genesis 6:1–2, 4–5)

Not all Bible scholars agree on what "sons of God" and "daughters of humans" mean. Some say the "sons of God" represent the godly line of Seth, while the "daughters of humans" represent the descendants of Cain. However, in other Scripture passages where the phrase "sons of God" is used, it means the angels (see Job 1:6 KJV, for example). So, it is possible this passage really means that the angels (fallen angels in this case) selected human women as mates. That could explain why their offspring were giants. It could even account for some of Greek mythology and for other ancient tales passed down by various civilizations throughout the generations. Why would the fallen angels do this? Remember the prophecy of Genesis 3:15, that the offspring of the woman would crush the old Serpent's head? Wouldn't it make sense, then, for Satan to hatch a plan to corrupt the "offspring," or descendants, of the woman so that the promised deliverer could never be born?

In any case, whether because of the rampant evil in the world, the corruption of the gene pool, or both, God decided to send a great flood to wipe out all inhabitants of the earth except for two representatives of every animal species, Noah, and the seven people in Noah's extended family. God instructed Noah to build a huge ark to house this surviving remnant. Noah did exactly as the Lord commanded, and the ark floated the survivors to safety as the floodwater ravaged the earth.

According to the New Testament, the flood and the ark each represent more than meets the eye. The book of 1 Peter tells us that the flood foreshadowed the baptism of Christian believers:

> In it [the ark] only a few people, eight in all, were saved through water, and this water symbolizes baptism that now saves you also—not the removal of dirt from the body but the pledge of a clear conscience toward God. It saves you by the resurrection of Jesus Christ. (1 Peter 3:20–21)

Noah and his family passed through the flood and into new life through the protection offered by the ark. Likewise, the Lord has given us the ability to become sons and daughters of God, passing through the waters of death and into new life by way of the shed blood of Jesus Christ, who is our protection against death and our shelter amid the storms of life. We recognize this new birth through the ceremony of baptism, which symbolizes our participation in the death and resurrection of Jesus Christ.

Jesus compared the suddenness of Noah's flood with the suddenness of His own return:

> As it was in the days of Noah, so it will be at the coming of the Son of Man. For in the days before the flood, people were eating and drinking, marrying and giving in marriage, up to the day Noah entered the ark; and they knew nothing about what would happen until the flood came and took them all away. That is how it will be at the coming of the Son of Man. (Matthew 24:37–39)

Christ's return will come at a time when many people will be absorbed in the simple pleasures of life, paying no heed to God's offer of salvation. Indeed, there will be scoffers who will completely dismiss the possibility of the Lord's return

(2 Peter 3:3–4). But there will be great destruction for those not ready for the second coming, just as there was destruction for those left outside the ark upon the arrival of the flood. The ark was God's one appointed means of salvation at the time of the flood. Those left outside were doomed to perish. Likewise, those who have not entered into the protection that only Christ has to offer will face judgment upon His return. This time, the judgment and destruction will come by fire instead of by water:

> By these waters also the world of that time was deluged and destroyed. By the same word the present heavens and earth are reserved for fire, being kept for the day of judgment and destruction of the ungodly. (2 Peter 3:6–7)

As we can see from these parallels, Noah's ark is another type of Jesus Christ. Further examination of the pertinent Scriptures reinforces this conclusion.

On three occasions, Noah sent out a dove to determine whether the floodwater had receded from the land. The dove came back empty-handed the first time, and returned with an olive branch the second time. The third time the dove was sent out, it never returned. Thousands of years later, as Jesus was being baptized in the Jordan River, John the Baptist "saw the Spirit of God descending like a dove and alighting on him" (Matthew 3:16).

We can observe a surprising parallel in these two episodes: During the "baptism" of Noah and his family in the flood, a fleshly dove ascended out of the ark in search of a home. During Jesus's baptism, a spiritual dove descended upon Him and found a home.

Thus, even when the Lord was destroying the old world with water, He was at the same time figuratively portraying the salvation of His people through Jesus the Messiah during the present world's destruction by fire. The lesson to be learned from this is quite clear: Jesus is our true Noah's ark, "who rescues us from the coming wrath" (1 Thessalonians 1:10). We must receive the protection He offers by acknowledging Him as Lord and Savior of our lives. Once He has become our Savior, we should heed the instructions contained in 2 Peter:

> You ought to live holy and godly lives as you look forward to the day of God and speed its coming. That day will bring about the destruction of the heavens by fire, and the elements will melt in the heat. But in keeping with his promise we are looking forward to a new heaven and a new earth, where righteousness dwells. (2 Peter 3:11–13)

Through Christ, our true Noah's ark, we will escape the future deluge of fire and dwell forever in the new earth as His people.

CHAPTER 6
Decoding the Life of Isaac

There are a number of Old Testament characters whose lives contain significant parallels to the life of Jesus. We have already noted many of these parallels in the case of Adam, and many additional characters will be examined over the course of this book.

As the case of Adam shows, these parallels often take the form of contrasts rather than similarities. For instance, both Adam and Jesus were tempted by Satan in the area of food—Adam with the forbidden fruit, and Jesus with the stones that could have been turned into bread. But Adam gave in to the temptation while Jesus successfully resisted. Contrasts such as this show us that the Old Testament characters were imperfect people who often made mistakes. Therefore, they could never be completely Christlike.

Yet, even in the contrasts, we can often observe an elegant symmetry between the Old and New Testaments, as the case of Adam demonstrates. The Lord often used the flaws of the Old Testament characters to emphasize the perfection of Jesus Christ. In contrast to Adam, however, Isaac appeared to live a relatively blameless life. For this reason, an examination of the life of Isaac in light of the life of Christ reveals more similarities than contrasts.

Some of the parallels between the lives of Isaac and Jesus have already been noted at the beginning of chapter 1. A more complete and thorough look at the life of Isaac will reveal even more New Testament similarities.

Isaac was the only son of Abraham and Sarah, whom God called to be the forebears of the Jewish people. The book of Genesis gives some notable facts about the circumstances surrounding Isaac's conception and birth. We find in chapter 18 the account of the Lord's visit to the parents-to-be. The Lord told Abraham in verse 10, "I will surely return to you about this time next year, and Sarah your wife will have a son."

This corresponds closely with Luke's account of the angelic announcement to Mary concerning the conception and birth of Jesus: "Do not be afraid, Mary, you have found favor with God. You will conceive and give birth to a son" (Luke 1:30–31).

Thus we see in each case that there was a divine revelation to the parents prior to the conception of the child. Further parallels become apparent as we continue our study of the Scriptures: "Now Sarah was listening at the entrance to the tent, which was behind him. Abraham and Sarah were already very old, and Sarah was past the age of childbearing" (Genesis 18:10–11).

The conception of Isaac was a miracle. So, of course, was the conception of Jesus: "This is how the birth of Jesus the Messiah came about. His mother Mary was pledged to be married to Joseph, but before they came together, she was found to be pregnant through the Holy Spirit" (Matthew 1:18).

In the case of Isaac, the Lord overcame the obstacle of extreme age to enable Sarah to conceive and give birth. In the case of Jesus, a virgin birth occurred. It is interesting to note the incredulous reactions of the mothers-to-be when told of the impending births: "So Sarah laughed to herself as she thought, 'After I am worn out and my lord is old, will I now have this pleasure?'" (Genesis 18:12.) Mary asked the angel incredulously, "How will this be ... since I am a virgin" (Luke 1:34)?

The replies in each case are noteworthy for their similarity: "Is anything too hard for the Lord?" asked the angel in Genesis 18:14. The angel's response to Mary in Luke's gospel was, "For with God nothing shall be impossible" (Luke 1:37 KJV).

Thus, a rhetorical question is asked in Genesis 18 and is answered in Luke 1.

Another common theme connecting the births of these two famous sons is the prenatal naming. In each case, the parents were given a name for their son and a brief description of the role he would play in God's plans: "Your wife Sarah will bear you a son, and you will call him Isaac. I will establish my covenant with him as an everlasting covenant for his descendants after him" (Genesis 17:19).

In Matthew 1, the angel explained to Joseph what was happening to Mary: "She will give birth to a son, and you are to give him the name Jesus, because he will save his people from their sins" (Matthew 1:21).

The parallels between these two lives continue into adulthood. In the near sacrifice of Isaac near Mount Moriah, we see foreshadowed the actual sacrifice of Jesus at Calvary. The account of the former incident in the book of Genesis describes the place where it was to occur and the manner in which it was to occur:

> Then God said, "Take your son, your only son, whom you love—Isaac—and go to the region of Moriah. Sacrifice him there as a burnt offering on a mountain I will show you." ... Abraham took the wood for the burnt offering and placed it on his son Isaac, and he himself carried the fire and the knife. (Genesis 22:2, 6)

According to the Lord's instructions, the sacrifice was to have taken place on one of the hills in the region of Mount Moriah. As Abraham and his party approached the place, Isaac himself bore the wood upon which he was to have been slain. Since Abraham was planning to stab his son with a knife, death by piercing was to have occurred.

Jesus bore His wooden cross to the place of His crucifixion (John 19:17). His hands and feet were pierced by nails as He was fastened to the cross, and a spear was thrust through His side (John 19:34).

As was the case in the account of Isaac's birth, a question is asked that echoes across the Scriptures and is finally answered in the New Testament two thousand years later: "'The fire and wood are here,' Isaac said, 'but where is the lamb for the burnt offering'" (Genesis 22:7)? "The next day John saw Jesus coming toward him and said, 'Look, the Lamb of God who takes away the sin of the world'" (John 1:29)!

A revealing passage in 2 Chronicles 3:1 provides further insight: "Then Solomon began to build the temple of the Lord in Jerusalem on Mount Moriah, where the Lord had appeared to his father David." This Scripture establishes the fact that Jerusalem was built on Mount Moriah. Since Jesus was crucified on a hill just outside Jerusalem, He, like Isaac, had His experience with death in "the region of Moriah." Therefore, at the time of Isaac's near sacrifice, the Lord led Abraham to the same area where, two thousand years later, Jesus was to be crucified.

Could it even have been the same hill? We cannot know this for certain, since the Bible is unclear as to which hill the Lord showed to Abraham. Jerusalem had not yet been built and the area was still a wilderness. But in view of how the Lord has used the Old Testament to foreshadow events in the New Testament, it would come as no surprise to me if the two places were identical.

At the conclusion of Isaac's dress rehearsal for Jesus's

crucifixion, the Lord abruptly halted the proceedings and drew Abraham's attention to a substitute: "There in a thicket he saw a ram caught by its horns. He went over and took the ram and sacrificed it as a burnt offering instead of his son" (Genesis 22:13).

At this point, the symbolism changed. The ram became a type of Christ, and Isaac began to foreshadow the believers whose punishment Jesus took.

There is more. Recall that as a result of God's curse upon the ground, the earth brought forth thorns and thistles (Genesis 3:17–18). Two thousand years later, Abraham saw a ram stuck in a thicket, its horns caught by the unruly tangle of thorns and thistles which the ground had brought forth. This ram slain in the place of Isaac bore, in a manner of speaking, a crown of thorns as it stood there entangled by its horns. The thorns were symbolic of the curses laid down by God in the book of Genesis.

Two thousand years after the sacrifice of this ram, Pilate's soldiers made a crown of thorns and placed it upon the head of Jesus, the true Lamb of God (John 19:2). Jesus, in wearing the crown of thorns, took upon Himself the curses of Genesis and washed them away with His own blood. Jesus then died in place of the spiritual sons of Abraham who believed in Him.

As the Genesis account of Isaac shows, the sacrificial death of Jesus was foreshadowed in detail in the Old Testament thousands of years before it actually happened. The Lord, in His wisdom and sovereignty, designed a symbolic passion play of the life and death of Jesus and wove it into the life of Isaac, and into the Biblical account of Isaac's life and near sacrifice. Many other such hidden passion plays exist in the Old Testament. As with the case of Jesus's miraculous signs, we may also say of these symbolic depictions, "These are written that you may believe that Jesus is the Messiah, the Son of God, and that by believing you may have life in his name" (John 20:31).

CHAPTER 7
Decoding the Life of Joseph

Joseph, like Isaac, was one of those rare Old Testament characters whose life, by all indications, was unmarred by significant blemish or scandal. Adam had handed the world over to Satan through his disobedience. Noah went on a drinking binge after the flood was over. Abraham lied to the king of Egypt concerning his relationship with his wife, Sarah. Moses's first recorded act was to slay a man. David committed adultery with Bathsheba and murdered her husband to cover up the act after she became pregnant. However, the Scriptures record no such blemish on Joseph's record. He was by all accounts a very righteous man.

Because of Joseph's righteousness, the Lord was able to use him mightily to rescue his family from famine. In the process, God made Joseph one of the most impressive types of Christ in the entire Old Testament.

The book of Genesis devotes several chapters to Joseph's life, starting with chapter 37. The youngest of the family, Joseph was the most beloved of Jacob's twelve children. His brothers detected this fact, however, and resented him for it. Adding fuel to the fire, Joseph had dreams of his whole family bowing down before him, and he was not bashful about sharing these dreams with them. The resentment that ensued grew to such an extent over time that Joseph's brothers were finally ready to kill him.

They saw their chance to get even one day when Jacob sent Joseph out into the countryside to find his brothers and report on how they were doing. Seeing him approach from afar, they conspired against him. Only Reuben's persuasiveness prevented Joseph from being killed. As it was, they cast Joseph alive into a pit and left the scene to debate his fate. They finally hatched a plan to sell him as a slave to a group of traveling Ishmaelites.

During his brothers' absence, however, Joseph was found and was spirited away by a group of Midianites, who themselves sold Joseph to the Ishmaelites. Upon finding Joseph gone from the pit, the brothers gave him up for lost and reported his death to Jacob.

Meanwhile, the Ishmaelites carried Joseph into Egypt and sold him into slavery. Joseph became a servant of the chief guard of the pharaoh. But the Lord gave Joseph favor in the sight of the guard, and the guard appointed Joseph steward over his entire household. This pattern was to be repeated several times in Joseph's life as he caught the attention of powerful men and gained their confidence.

Joseph's new career suffered a significant setback when he was falsely accused by the chief guard's wife and then thrown into prison. But the Lord continued to favor him even in prison.

In due course, Joseph found himself imprisoned with two of the pharaoh's chief servants, the butler and the baker. After Joseph had successfully interpreted their dreams, the butler was released. The butler eventually informed the pharaoh of Joseph's abilities, when the pharaoh himself needed to have a dream interpreted. The pharaoh sent for Joseph, heard Joseph's interpretation, and accepted it as valid. He then set Joseph over his entire kingdom to prepare it for the catastrophe Joseph had predicted: seven years of plenty followed by seven years of severe famine.

The famine occurred just as Joseph had predicted, and

its effect was felt throughout the Middle East. Egypt, under Joseph's rule, had set aside grain from the years of plenty and was able to draw upon the supply to survive. The surrounding regions, including the land where Joseph's family lived, were far less prepared.

Finally, Jacob's sons were forced to travel to Egypt to purchase grain in order to survive. There, they bowed down before their long-lost brother Joseph, who gave them the grain they needed but who hid his identity from them until their second visit. Finally, he was able to hide his identity no longer. They had a tearful reunion, at which time Joseph invited his family to move to Egypt. Joseph forgave his brothers and pointed out to them God's hidden purpose in bringing him to Egypt: to make a way for them to survive the famine.

As is the case with Isaac, there are aspects of Joseph's life that resemble and foreshadow the life of Christ. In Isaac's case, the similarities reside in the circumstances surrounding his birth and his near sacrifice. In Joseph's case, the similarities reside in his early ministry to his brothers, his apparent humiliation and defeat, his attainment of authority and rulership, and his self-revelation to his brothers. Each one of these will be examined in turn.

Joseph's early ministry to his brothers resembled Christ's ministry in certain key aspects. In Jacob's love for Joseph (Genesis 37:3) we see foreshadowed God's expression of love for His only begotten Son (Matthew 3:17). Joseph was sent by his father on a mission to visit his brothers, who had wandered far from home (Genesis 37:12–13). Likewise, the heavenly Father sent the Son on a mission to "go after the lost sheep" of Israel (Luke 15:4). Joseph encountered hatred and unbelief from his brothers (Genesis 37:4–5). Likewise, Jesus's fellow Israelites hated Him without reason (John 15:25). Not even His own brothers believed in Him (John 7:5). Joseph's brothers asked the sneering question, "Do you intend to reign over us" (Genesis 37:8)? The Israelites encountered this same question with regard to Jesus, and their response to Jesus (in a parable) was, "We don't want this man to be our king" (Luke 19:14).

In both cases the extreme negative reactions eventually turned violent and resulted in the apparent disgrace and defeat of both Joseph and Jesus. The Scriptures tell us Joseph was conspired against (Genesis 37:18), stripped (Genesis 37:23), sold for twenty pieces of silver (Genesis 37:28), and turned over to the Gentiles (Genesis 37:28). Likewise, Jesus was conspired against (Matthew 27:1), sold for thirty pieces of silver (Matthew 26:14–15), turned over to the Gentiles (Matthew 27:2), and stripped (Matthew 27:28). Joseph's brothers cast him into a cistern and then sat down to eat (Genesis 37:24–25). Jesus's adversaries hung Him on a cross and then sat down to watch (Matthew 27:35–36).

Joseph was made a servant (Genesis 39:1–2), was falsely accused (Genesis 39:11–15), and was placed in prison with the pharaoh's prisoners (Genesis 39:20). His feet were bound with shackles (Psalm 105:18). Jesus "made himself nothing by taking the very nature of a servant" (Philippians 2:7), was falsely accused (Matthew 26:59–61), and "was numbered with the transgressors" (Isaiah 53:12). His hands and feet were pierced (Psalm 22:16).

While he was in prison, Joseph encountered two officers who had done wrong (Genesis 40:2–4). To one of them he gave a message of life (Genesis 40:13). While He was on the cross, Jesus encountered two men who had done wrong (Luke 23:32). To one of them He gave an assurance that he would be with Him in paradise (Luke 23:43).

After Joseph and Jesus appeared to be totally defeated, God raised each of them up and conferred great authority and rulership upon them.

Concerning Joseph, Pharaoh said:

> "Can we find anyone like this man, one in whom is the spirit of God?" Then Pharaoh said

to Joseph, "Since God has made all this known to you, there is no one so discerning and wise as you. You shall be in charge of my palace, and all my people are to submit to your orders. Only with respect to the throne will I be greater than you." So Pharaoh said to Joseph, "I hereby put you in charge of the whole land of Egypt." (Genesis 41:38–41)

Similarly, the Scriptures read, "God anointed Jesus of Nazareth with the Holy Spirit and power" (Acts 10:38), and "all the treasures of wisdom and knowledge" are hidden in Christ (Colossians 2:3). "God placed all things under his feet" (Ephesians 1:22), but "this does not include God himself" (1 Corinthians 15:27).

Pharaoh ordered the people to "bow the knee" whenever Joseph passed by (Genesis 41:43 KJV). Similarly, Scripture tells us that "at the name of Jesus every knee should bow" (Philippians 2:10).

Scripture tells us that the grain Joseph stored up "was so much that he stopped keeping records because it was beyond measure" (Genesis 41:49). Scripture also speaks of "the boundless riches of Christ" (Ephesians 3:8). When the people needed grain, the pharaoh said, "Go to Joseph and do what he tells you" (Genesis 41:55). This reminds us of the wedding at Cana. When the wine was gone, Mary said to the servants, "Do whatever he tells you" (John 2:5). The respective results were that the people received their grain and the wedding guests received their wine.

When Joseph was finally reunited with his brothers, "they did not recognize him" (Genesis 42:8). Joseph gave them "as much food as they [could] carry" (Genesis 44:1). In a similar way, when the resurrected Jesus found His disciples fishing, "the disciples did not realize that it was Jesus" (John 21:4). They nevertheless took His suggestion, and when they had cast their nets on the right side of the boat, "they were unable to haul the net in because of the large number of fish" (John 21:6).

Finally, Joseph "made himself known to his brothers" (Genesis 45:1). He said, "You can see for yourselves, and so can my brother Benjamin, that it is really I who am speaking to you" (Genesis 45:12). Similarly, the resurrected Jesus finally made Himself known to His disciples. He said, "Look at my hands and my feet. It is I myself!" (Luke 24:39).

Joseph nicely summed up for his brothers the providential meaning and purpose of the ordeal they had put him through:

> And now, do not be distressed and do not be angry with yourselves for selling me here, because it was to save lives that God sent me ahead of you. For two years now there has been famine in the land, and for the next five years there will be no plowing and reaping. But God sent me ahead of you to preserve for you a remnant on earth and to save your lives by a great deliverance. (Genesis 45:5–7)

Jesus also nicely summed up for His disciples the providential meaning and purpose of His suffering and death:

> Then he opened their minds so they could understand the Scriptures. He told them, "This is what is written: The Messiah will suffer and rise from the dead on the third day, and repentance for the forgiveness of sins will be preached in his name to all nations, beginning at Jerusalem." (Luke 24:45–47)

Figure 3 sums up these many similarities in a side-by-side comparison. It is abundantly clear that Joseph's life extensively foreshadowed the life of Jesus Christ, both in the sufferings each endured and in the glory that was to follow. The only significant exception to these parallels is that Joseph was not required to lay down his life.

FIGURE 3:

JOSEPH AND JESUS

PARALLELS IN THEIR DEFINING MOMENTS

JOSEPH		JESUS
GENESIS 37:3	LOVED BY HIS FATHER	MATTHEW 3:17
GENESIS 37:12-13	FATHER SENT SON ON A MISSION	JOHN 8:18
GENESIS 37:4-5	BROTHERS HATED HIM FOR NO REASON	JOHN 15:25
GENESIS 37:8	REJECTED RULER	LUKE 19:14 (Parable)
GENESIS 37:18	CONSPIRED AGAINST	MATTHEW 27:1
GENESIS 37:23	STRIPPED	MATTHEW 27:28
GENESIS 37:28	SOLD FOR PIECES OF SILVER	MATTHEW 26:14-15
GENESIS 37:28	TURNED OVER TO GENTILES	MATTHEW 27:2
GENESIS 37:24-25	PERPETRATORS SAT DOWN	MATTHEW 27:35-36
GENESIS 39:11-15	FALSELY ACCUSED	MATTHEW 26:59-61
GENESIS 39:20	NUMBERED WITH THE TRANSGRESSORS	ISAIAH 53:12
GENESIS 40:2-4	TWO WRONGDOERS	LUKE 23:32
GENESIS 40:13	TO ONE A MESSAGE OF LIFE	LUKE 23:43
GENESIS 41:38-41	SPIRIT FILLED	ACTS 10:38
"	WISDOM AND KNOWLEDGE	COLOSSIANS 2:3
"	OVER ALL . . .	EPHESIANS 1:22
"	. . . EXCEPT PHAROAH/THE FATHER	I CORINTHIANS 15:27
GENESIS 41:43	BOW THE KNEE	PHILIPPIANS 2:10
GENESIS 41:49	RICHES BEYOND MEASURE	EPHESIANS 3:8
GENESIS 41:55	"DO WHAT HE TELLS YOU"	JOHN 2:5
GENESIS 42:8	DID NOT RECOGNIZE HIM	JOHN 21:4
GENESIS 44:1	AS MUCH AS THEY COULD CARRY	JOHN 21:6
GENESIS 45:1	MADE HIMSELF KNOWN	LUKE 24:31
GENESIS 45:12	"IT IS I"	LUKE 24:39
GENESIS 45:5-7	HIS ORDEAL BROUGHT ABOUT A GREAT DELIVERANCE	LUKE 24:46-47

CHAPTER 8
Decoding the Life of Moses

The heroes of the Old Testament had their flaws just as we do today. Therefore, we should not expect them to be perfect types of Christ. But even in their flaws we can often learn something about Jesus, for the Lord is able to use these flaws to magnify and highlight the perfection of Christ. We can see several examples of this in Moses's life. In this chapter, we will examine both the similarities and the contrasts between Moses and Jesus.

First we will examine some of the similarities. The danger Moses faced as a baby was the very same one Jesus faced: a campaign of infanticide directed against male Israelite babies by a paranoid monarch (compare Exodus 1:22 and Matthew 2:16). In each case, the monarch's attempts on the life of Israel's deliverer failed because of God's divine protection. Thus, Moses was raised in the pharaoh's own household yet grew up to become one of Israel's greatest deliverers.

But after four hundred years of slavery in Egypt, the Israelites seemed no more inclined to accept their God-appointed deliverer than they had been when Joseph first revealed his dreams to his indignant and unreceptive brothers.

Exodus 2 tells us that when Moses was fully grown up, he went out to visit his Hebrew brothers, who were working for the Egyptians as slaves. Seeing an Egyptian mistreating one of the Hebrews, Moses rose up in anger and killed the

Egyptian. Moses thought his deed had gone undetected, but word of it somehow leaked out, first to his fellow Hebrews and then to the Egyptians.

The Hebrews were apparently unimpressed. When Moses tried the next day to stop two Hebrews from fighting, one of them asked, "Who made you ruler and judge over us? Are you thinking of killing me as you killed the Egyptian" (Exodus 2:14)? Realizing his deed had been discovered, Moses fled into the wilderness.

Thus, like Joseph before him and Christ after him, Moses "came to that which was his own, but his own did not receive him" (John 1:11). Moses settled in the land of Midian and took a Gentile wife. He worked as a shepherd for his father-in-law, Jethro, the priest of Midian.

After forty years of tending sheep in the wilderness, Moses, at eighty years old, must have seen the pharaoh's household in Egypt as nothing more than a dim memory of a bygone era. But the most important period in Moses's life was still to come. As he was tending the sheep one day, the Lord appeared to him in a burning bush. The Lord commissioned him to lead the Israelites out of Egypt. Moses overcame his initial reluctance and returned to Egypt armed with the power and authority God had given him. Upon his return, he found that conditions for the Israelites were even worse than when he had left them. The Israelites were finally ready to follow Moses out of Egypt, and they submitted to his leadership. After a long struggle with the pharaoh, one punctuated by numerous signs and wonders from God, Moses succeeded in leading the Israelites out of Egypt.

After all his years as a lonely shepherd, Moses now found himself leading a nation of people. As the Israelites wandered in the wilderness for forty years, the education Moses had received while in the pharaoh's household must have come in handy. But he probably depended even more heavily upon the principles he had learned while tending sheep. The Israelites started their journey as a whining and insecure group of former slaves who still had a slave mentality. When they entered the Promised Land, they were no longer recognizable as the group that had set out from Egypt forty years earlier. They were a lean, tough band of warriors who had a strong faith in God.

In a similar way, Jesus "the good shepherd" (John 10:14) is performing mighty works in the lives of His people today, for "we are God's handiwork" (Ephesians 2:10). Moreover, we are assured that "he who began a good work in [us] will carry it on to completion until the day of Christ Jesus" (Philippians 1:6).

After his long absence, the Israelites finally accepted Moses, as they ultimately had accepted Joseph. Jesus too began a long absence after most of the Israelites rejected Him as their Lord and Savior on the initial encounter with Him. This bodily absence continues to this day, though He is with the Christian believer through the Holy Spirit. As Moses took a Gentile bride during his absence, so also has Christ taken for His bride the predominantly Gentile church. One day, however, Israel will be reunited with her Messiah and will accept Him. As the Scriptures point out,

> Israel has experienced a hardening in part until the full number of the Gentiles has come in. And in this way all Israel will be saved. As it is written: "The deliverer will come from Zion; he will turn godlessness away from Jacob." (Romans 11:25–26)

On that day, says Zechariah 12:10 prophetically, "They will look on me, the one they have pierced, and they will mourn for him as one mourns for an only child, and grieve bitterly for him as one grieves for a firstborn son."

To gain a fuller appreciation of the parallels between Jesus and Moses, it is necessary also to point out some of the contrasts between them. As we have seen, Moses's first recorded public act was to kill a man (Exodus 2:12). However, Jesus's first recorded public act (in the book of Mark, at least) was to heal a man by casting out an evil spirit (Mark 1:23–26). Moses broke the law into fragments with his hands (Exodus 32:19), but Jesus kept the law perfectly in His heart. Moses turned water into blood, but Jesus turned water into wine. Jesus Himself pointed out the contrast between the bread provided under Moses's leadership and the bread He provides:

> I am the bread of life. Your ancestors ate the manna in the wilderness, yet they died. But here is the bread that comes down from heaven, which anyone may eat and not die. I am the living bread that came down from heaven. Whoever eats this bread will live forever. (John 6:48–51)

All of these contrasts allow Jesus's perfection to stand out, setting Him apart from anyone who had come before Him. As the Scripture points out, "For the law was given through Moses; grace and truth came through Jesus Christ" (John 1:17). On the day the law was given, three thousand people were killed because of their disobedience (Exodus 32:28), but on the day the Holy Spirit was given, three thousand people were saved because of God's forgiveness (Acts 2:41). As 2 Corinthians 3:6 explains, "For the letter kills, but the Spirit gives life."

Aside from all of the specific similarities and contrasts related above, there is an interesting collection of more general parallels between Moses and Jesus. These more general parallels relate to the offices or functions performed by both Moses and Jesus, such as the office of shepherd, as noted previously.

Moses was the foremost deliverer of the Old Testament.

In this office, he is a strong type of Christ, the Savior of the world.

In addition, Moses was a prophet, as was Jesus. Moses prophetically described this similarity between himself and the Jewish Messiah when he told the Israelites, "The Lord your God will raise up for you a prophet like me from among you, from your fellow Israelites. You must listen to him" (Deuteronomy 18:15). Though many did not listen to Jesus, some did. "I can see that you are a prophet," said the Samaritan woman at the well (John 4:19).

Scripture states that "Moses and Aaron were among [God's] priests" (Psalm 99:6). Scripture also states of the Messiah, "You are a priest forever, in the order of Melchizedek" (Psalm 110:4). Thus Moses and Jesus shared the office of priest. But there is a critical difference between Jesus and the priests of the Old Testament: "Now there have been many of those priests, since death prevented them from continuing in office; but because Jesus lives forever, he has a permanent priesthood" (Hebrews 7:23–24). Thus, once again a contrast is evident in the midst of a parallel, but the contrast serves to accentuate the perfection of Jesus.

The office of judge is another office shared by both Moses and Jesus. Exodus 18:13 explains, "The next day Moses took his seat to serve as judge for the people, and they stood around him from morning till evening." In John 5:26–27, Jesus explains, "For as the Father has life in himself, so he has granted the Son also to have life in himself. And he has given him authority to judge because he is the Son of Man."

Jesus and Moses also shared the office of mediator:

> Anyone inquiring of the Lord would go to the tent of meeting outside the camp. And whenever Moses went out to the tent, all the people rose and stood at the entrances to their tents, watching Moses until he entered the tent. As

> Moses went into the tent, the pillar of cloud would come down and stay at the entrance, while the Lord spoke with Moses. (Exodus 33:7–9)

Thus, the people of Israel had no direct, face-to-face dealings with God; instead, they relied upon Moses as their link with God. Today, we have a more perfect mediator in Jesus Christ. As 1 Timothy 2:5 explains, "For there is one God and one mediator between God and mankind, the man Christ Jesus."

Perhaps one of the most crucial offices held by Moses was the office of intercessor. While Moses was on Mount Sinai receiving instructions from God, the Israelites made a golden calf and began to worship it. Were it not for Moses's intercession, the Lord would have wiped out the Israelites and started over again with just Moses (see Exodus 32:7–14).

On another occasion, when the Israelites were fighting the Amalekites, "as long as Moses held up his hands, the Israelites were winning, but whenever he lowered his hands, the Amalekites were winning" (Exodus 17:11). When Moses grew weary, his hands had to be held up. In due course, the Israelites prevailed (Exodus 17:12–13).

In a similar way, Jesus intercedes for Christian believers today: "Therefore he is able to save completely those who come to God through him, because he always lives to intercede for them" (Hebrews 7:25).

Each of the Old Testament characters examined so far has areas of his life in which Christ is foreshadowed in many significant ways. These areas differ from one character to the next. Isaac foreshadowed Christ in the circumstances surrounding his birth and his near sacrifice. Joseph's life foreshadowed Christ's sufferings and glory. Moses's life foreshadowed many of the offices held by Christ: deliverer, shepherd, prophet, priest, judge, mediator, and intercessor, among others.

The overall message that is beginning to emerge is that Jesus Christ is the focal point of the entire Bible. All of God's dealings with the Israelites were conducted with Christ in mind. We can see Jesus of Nazareth emerging now as the pivotal figure in human history.

CHAPTER 9
Decoding the First Passover and the Exodus

Suppose you were a slave in the land of Egypt and had been one all your life. The work was hard, but you were accustomed to it. You were fed regularly and given adequate shelter from the elements. Your father was a slave also, as had been his father before him.

Then suppose one day there appeared an individual with an incredible story to tell. This story touched upon an old tradition passed down from generation to generation among your people. It concerned a God who had dealt with your ancestors some four hundred years ago, a length of time roughly equal to the time span from the arrival of the first English settlers in America to the present. This God, the person said, appeared in a burning bush and spoke with him, and now wants to deliver you and your community out of slavery and bring you into a new land selected specifically for your people.

If you are like many people, you may think that this sounds too good to be true. Besides, you are accustomed to life here. You reflect that you would probably not know what to do with yourself once you had left.

This was the situation faced by the Israelites after living in Egypt for 430 years, most of those years as slaves. It is not unlike the situation faced by people today when confronted with the gospel of Jesus Christ. Each individual has to make a choice. The Scriptures present it as a choice between slavery in Satan's kingdom and freedom in Christ's kingdom. Yet many people are content to remain in darkness, preferring the bondage to which they are accustomed over the freedom to which they are unaccustomed.

One of the miracles of the exodus was the parting of the Red Sea. But it was no less a miracle that the Israelites believed Moses and allowed him to lead them out of Egypt. That said, the Lord had prepared the way. The Israelites were aware they would one day depart from Egypt, for Joseph had told them so:

> Then Joseph said to his brothers, "I am about to die. But God will surely come to your aid and take you up out of this land to the land he promised on oath to Abraham, Isaac and Jacob." And Joseph made the sons of Israel swear an oath and said, "God will surely come to your aid, and then you must carry my bones up from this place." (Genesis 50:24–25)

When the appointed time came for the Israelites to leave Egypt, the Lord brought forth great signs and wonders to confirm to the Israelites that it was indeed time to leave. The most dramatic signs were the ten plagues inflicted upon the Egyptians. These plagues are prophetic in nature, for they appear to closely resemble the plagues that will befall the whole world during the great tribulation. These latter plagues are described in the book of Revelation.

However, the event packed with the most prophetic significance was the introduction of a ceremony that came to be known as the Passover. The Lord had extended His hand of protection to the Israelites during the first nine plagues. Likewise, the Lord devised a plan to protect His people during the tenth plague.

As explained in Exodus 12, the Lord gave Moses clear

instructions: Each household was to select a firstborn male lamb without blemish. These lambs would be kept until the fourteenth day of the month and then slaughtered by the whole community of Israel in the evening. Each Israelite household was to take the blood of the lamb and apply it to the top of their door frame and to both sides. None of the lamb's bones were to be broken. The lamb would then be roasted over fire with bitter herbs and eaten along with the bitter herbs and unleavened bread. The meal was to be eaten in haste, with each Israelite dressed and ready for an imminent departure.

The Israelites followed Moses's instructions, though they could not have understood the meaning of all of the symbols. John the Baptist, however, understood them well. As he saw Jesus approaching, he exclaimed, "Look, the Lamb of God, who takes away the sin of the world" (John 1:29)! The lamb, like Jesus, was killed with the collaboration of the entire community of Israel. And like Jesus, none of its bones were broken (John 19:36).

The blood of the lamb in the doorway formed the shape of a cross. If Jesus could have been placed in one of those doorways while He was on the cross, the blood from His pierced hands and His thorn-scratched head would have corresponded exactly to the blood on the sides and top of the door frame.

Because of the blood of the lamb, the terrible plague could not harm members of the Israelite households. But each Egyptian household was to lose its firstborn. Thus, death had no power over the Israelites because of the blood of the lamb.

In a corresponding way, death has no power over the Christian believer because of the blood of Jesus. As Jesus told His disciples, "Whoever eats my flesh and drinks my blood has eternal life, and I will raise them up at the last day. For my flesh is real food and my blood is real drink" (John 6:54–55).

At the appointed time, each Egyptian household did indeed suffer the loss of its firstborn child. However, the

Israelites were spared this loss of life. When the pharaoh realized what had happened, he immediately expelled the Israelites from the land of Egypt. The Israelites left for the wilderness in great haste.

Once again, the pharaoh changed his mind, but this time it was too late to stop the departing Israelites. When Pharaoh's pursuing armies trapped the Israelites against the Red Sea, Moses, acting on the Lord's instructions, stretched forth his hand over the sea. The sea then parted to allow the Israelites through. After the Israelites had reached the opposite shore, the sea closed up again, swallowing the pursuing Egyptians (Exodus 14).

There was great rejoicing among the Israelites as they realized they were free at last. Moreover, the Lord stayed with them and continued to guide them. The Lord's method of guidance was as follows:

> By day the Lord went ahead of them in a pillar of cloud to guide them on their way and by night in a pillar of fire to give them light, so that they could travel by day or night. Neither the pillar of cloud by day nor the pillar of fire by night left its place in front of the people. (Exodus 13:21–22)

The New Testament sheds some additional light on the meaning behind God's techniques of rescuing and guiding the Israelites:

> For I do not want you to be ignorant of the fact, brothers and sisters, that our ancestors were all under the cloud and that they all passed through the sea. They were all baptized into Moses in the cloud and in the sea. (1 Corinthians 10:1–2)

Decoding Bible Messages

We can see that the Lord had two forms of baptism in mind when He brought the Israelites out of Egypt. Scripture supports the idea that baptism takes two forms, as Acts 1:5 tells us, "For John baptized with water, but in a few days you will be baptized with the Holy Spirit."

Both of these baptisms are symbolized in the exodus. The passage of the Israelites through the water foreshadowed water baptism, the act by which Christian believers acknowledge they have accepted Christ and have passed from death into eternal life.

The gift of the pillar of cloud foreshadowed the baptism of the Holy Spirit. The purpose of the cloud was to provide the Israelites with an ever-present source of guidance and reassurance during their journey through the wilderness. Likewise, the Holy Spirit, whom Jesus called the Counselor, serves the same purpose for the Christian during life's journeys: "But when he, the Spirit of truth, comes, he will guide you into all the truth. He will not speak on his own; he will speak only what he hears, and he will tell you what is yet to come" (John 16:13).

Those who have not yet given themselves to Christ are like the enslaved Israelites in Egypt serving an evil pharaoh while waiting for their deliverance: "As for you, you were dead in your transgressions and sins, in which you used to live when you followed the ways of this world and of the ruler of the kingdom of the air" (Ephesians 2:1–2).

Those who have accepted the call of Jesus Christ by faith have been rescued from Satan's kingdom by an act of God even more powerful than the one whereby He rescued the Israelites from Egypt: "For he [the Father] has rescued us from the dominion of darkness and brought us into the kingdom of the Son he loves" (Colossians 1:13).

But the parallels extend beyond this. Soon after the Israelites left Egypt, they became fearful and homesick. Many of them wanted to turn back.

John A. Mapp Jr.

Christians are subject to similar temptations. Once we have been saved, we Christians often have a tendency to look back and "long for the flesh pots of Egypt" just like the Israelites did before us. We tend to become entangled again in the law, or entangled again with sin. The Scriptures urge us to press on just as Moses urged his own people to press on: "It is for freedom that Christ has set us free. Stand firm, then, and do not let yourselves be burdened again by a yoke of slavery" (Galatians 5:1).

CHAPTER 10
Decoding the Wilderness Years: Part 1

After their sudden departure from Egypt, the Israelites entered the wilderness utterly at God's mercy and were forced to rely upon Him completely for their every need. But this must have been exactly how God wanted it, for, as He later told the apostle Paul, "My power is made perfect in weakness" (2 Corinthians 12:9). As a result, some of the greatest miracles of the Old Testament occurred while the Israelites were wandering in the wilderness, totally dependent upon God.

This dependence upon God extended even to matters as basic as the water supply. After the drowning of the pharaoh's armies and the great celebration that followed, the Israelites were confronted with the daily realities of life in the wilderness as they were forced to travel three days without water. When they finally came to an oasis, they found the water too bitter to drink. By this time, the euphoria of three days prior had given way to anger and disillusionment. They named the oasis Marah, meaning "bitterness."

As the Israelites approached the point of rebellion, Moses cried out to the Lord for help. The Lord showed Moses a tree and instructed him to cut it down and cast it into the water. When Moses did this, the water became sweet. The Israelites drank their fill, replenished their supply, and resumed their journey (Exodus 15:22–27).

The deeper meaning of this episode hinges on the meaning of the bitter water. It most likely represents death. The account of Noah's ark and the book of Jonah both bear out this interpretation, for water is clearly associated with death in these passages (see, for example, Jonah 2:1–6).

The tree appears to represent Christ, who was cast into the waters of death on our behalf. The result was that the bitterness, or destructiveness, of death was removed: "I will deliver this people from the power of the grave; I will redeem them from death. Where, O death, are your plagues? Where, O grave, is your destruction" (Hosea 13:14)?

Soon after this experience with water, the Israelites found themselves in need of food. Once again, their initial reaction showed a total lack of faith in God, even though God had just intervened miraculously to bring them water. They accused Moses of taking them out into the wilderness only to let them starve to death. They complained that they had been better off in Egypt where they had been fed regularly. Once again, Moses took the problem to God, who provided a solution: manna from heaven. This bread-like substance appeared every morning for the Israelites to gather, and it sustained them throughout their travels in the wilderness. It is described in the book of Numbers:

> The manna was like coriander seed and looked like resin. The people went around gathering it, and then ground it in a hand mill or crushed it in a mortar. They cooked it in a pot or made it into loaves. And it tasted like something made with olive oil. When the dew settled on the camp at night, the manna also came down. (Numbers 11:7–9)

The word *manna* means "what is it?" The Israelites never completely answered their own question, but there arose a widespread belief among them that when the Messiah came He would again provide them with this manna. When Jesus fed the five thousand near the shores of the Sea of Galilee, the Jews were naturally reminded of the manna and were curious to know if Jesus would likewise provide it (John 6:30–31). Jesus responded that He Himself was the Bread of Life, and He elaborated as follows:

> Your ancestors ate the manna in the wilderness, yet they died. But here is the bread that comes down from heaven, which anyone may eat and not die. I am the living bread that came down from heaven. Whoever eats this bread will live forever. This bread is my flesh, which I will give for the life of the world. (John 6:49–51)

Thus, in the manna from heaven we see foreshadowed Jesus Himself, who, once again, is the perfect fulfillment of that which had imperfectly symbolized Him many years before.

After further travels, the Israelites once again found themselves sorely in need of water. They were encamped in a place called Rephidim, where there was no water to drink. Moses cried out to the Lord as the people once again approached the point of mutiny. The Lord intervened again, but in an even more miraculous way than the first time. He gave these instructions to Moses:

> Go out in front of the people. Take with you some of the elders of Israel and take in your hand the staff with which you struck the Nile, and go. I will stand there before you by the rock at Horeb. Strike the rock, and water will come out of it for the people to drink. (Exodus 17:5–6)

Moses did as the Lord commanded him, and the water gushed forth directly from the rock.

The symbolism intended by the Holy Spirit is clearly explained in 1 Corinthians 10:3–4: "They all ate the same spiritual food and drank the same spiritual drink; for they drank from the spiritual rock that accompanied them, and that rock was Christ."

Jesus Himself traveled through the wilderness with the Israelites, revealing Himself to them through types such as the manna and the rock that brought forth water. The use of the rock that gave water as a symbol for Jesus seems especially appropriate in light of other Scripture passages that describe Him, some in the Old Testament and some in the New Testament. One such Old Testament passage is found in Jeremiah: "My people have committed two sins: They have forsaken me, the spring of living water, and have dug their own cisterns, broken cisterns that cannot hold water" (Jeremiah 2:13). This passage clearly presents Jesus as the source of living water. Another passage is found in Isaiah 53:12, which states prophetically that Jesus "poured out his life unto death" to atone for our sins.

It is striking to find such great truths of the Christian faith in the Old Testament. These passages clearly show the deeper meaning of the smitten rock that brought forth water. But as we search the New Testament, we find that the parallels become even more literal and astonishing. As Jesus was hanging on the cross, the Roman soldiers inspected His body and found Him dead. After this it is written, "One of the soldiers pierced Jesus's side with a spear, bringing a sudden flow of blood and water" (John 19:34).

Now, Jesus had a very rough time at the hand of Roman soldiers, both before and during His crucifixion. In fact, if a group of soldiers did to someone today what was done to Jesus back then, we would call it an atrocity. Moreover, soldiers generally do not act of their own accord; they follow orders and they have a chain of command. The Roman soldiers who beat Jesus, hung Him on the cross, and stabbed Him in the side with a spear had a leader, and they were operating under that leader's direction. The leader of a group of a hundred Roman soldiers was called a "centurion," and there was one present at the crucifixion.

Now let's fast-forward a few years. Acts 10 describes how the Lord gave Peter a vision and told him not to call "impure" that which the Lord had cleansed. The Lord was ready to extend salvation to the Gentiles and to pour out His Holy Spirit upon them. Whom did our Lord choose first from among all of the Gentiles? The first one among the Gentiles to have the living water of the Holy Spirit poured out upon him was Cornelius, a Roman centurion! It was Roman soldiers who had struck the Rock of Ages, and yet the Lord poured out His Holy Spirit upon a Roman centurion and his family! No wonder the Scriptures tell us that the love of Christ surpasses knowledge (Ephesians 3:19).

The final prophetic fulfillment of this episode is found in the book of Revelation:

> Then the angel showed me the river of the water of life, as clear as crystal, flowing from the throne of God and of the Lamb down the middle of the great street of the city. ... The Spirit and the bride say, "Come!" And let the one who hears say, "Come!" Let the one who is thirsty come; and let the one who wishes take the free gift of the water of life. (Revelation 22:1–2, 17)

Thus from a single episode in the Israelites' wilderness years, we are able to see symbolized several of the details of Jesus's death on the cross and its aftermath; the profound love of God; and some of the great doctrines of the Christian faith.

As one additional benefit, this view of the smitten rock helps us to understand why God did not allow Moses to lead the Israelites into the Promised Land. On a subsequent occasion when the Israelites needed water, the Lord again gave Moses instructions to obtain water from a rock. But this time Moses only had to *speak* to the rock to obtain the water. According to Numbers 20:8, the Lord told Moses, "Take the staff, and you and your brother Aaron gather the assembly together. Speak to that rock before their eyes and it will pour out its water." But instead of speaking to the rock, Moses angrily exclaimed, "Listen, you rebels, must we bring you water out of this rock" (Numbers 20:10)? Then Moses struck the rock with his staff not once, but twice.

Although God honored Moses's authority and allowed the rock to bring forth water, He was so displeased with Moses that He forbade him to lead the Israelites into the Promised Land. Years later, Moses died, with the Promised Land visible across the Jordan River but just out of his grasp.

Why was Moses's mistake serious enough to warrant this degree of punishment? One answer, no doubt, is that any act of disobedience against God is a serious matter. But there is more to it than that. Moses had spoiled one of God's types. Since the rock represented Christ, it had to be struck only once to make the water available for the entire journey, just as Jesus had to be crucified only once in order to bring us eternal salvation. As the book of Hebrews tells us,

> Nor did he enter heaven to offer himself again and again, the way the high priest enters the Most Holy Place every year with blood that is not his own. Otherwise Christ would have had to suffer many times since the creation of the world. But he has appeared once for all at the culmination of the ages to do away with sin by the sacrifice of himself. (Hebrews 9:25–26)

Thus, after the rock had been struck once, all Moses had to do in order to obtain more water was to speak to it. This is analogous to prayer in the life of a Christian. But in striking the rock again, Moses was in effect "crucifying the Son of God all over again and subjecting him to public disgrace" (Hebrews 6:6). This is certainly not the imagery God had intended.

The implications are clear. God took great care to build into the history of His people many prophetic portraits of the coming Messiah. He attached great importance to their accuracy and did not want them tampered with. When Moses spoiled one of these prophetic portraits, he incurred God's penalty and died before he could enter the Promised Land.

Whatever became of Moses? Did God just throw him into the dustbin of history? No. Nothing is as relentless as God's love and forgiveness, which can triumph over all sin. More than a thousand years later, Jesus led a small group of disciples to the top of a mountain. There He was transfigured (Matthew 17:1–3). His face became as bright as the sun and His garments shone brilliantly. And there by His side in the Promised Land stood two men: one of them was Elijah; the other, Moses.

CHAPTER 11
Decoding the Wilderness Years: Part 2

As the preceding chapter shows, God faithfully provided for the basic physical needs of His people during their forty years in the wilderness. This is not to say that the Israelites lived lives of luxury during their travels. It was a time of testing and refinement for them. A nation was to be built out of a timid and complaining band of ex-slaves. But God must have known the right combination of abundance and austerity, for the people who finally massed on the east bank of the Jordan River in preparation for the invasion of the Promised Land were completely different from the people who had emerged from Egypt forty years before. The torch had been passed to a new generation. Moses had just died, and the Israelites were now led by Joshua. (Recall that Moses had been forbidden to lead the people into the Promised Land because he had struck the rock twice.)

As part of that testing and refining process, God's provision for the Israelites covered areas such as healing, guidance, and instruction in the law, in addition to His providing for their physical needs. Thus God progressively revealed Himself to the Israelites during their travels so that they would be ready to serve Him when they became established in their new nation.

After the Israelites left Egypt, and shortly after their encounter with the bitter waters of Marah, the Lord brought forth a message to His people:

> If you listen carefully to the Lord your God and do what is right in his eyes, if you pay attention to his commands and keep all his decrees, I will not bring on you any of the diseases I brought on the Egyptians, for I am the Lord who heals you. (Exodus 15:26)

The mercurial Israelites alternately heeded and ignored this promise throughout their travels. On one occasion, as they traveled along the route from Mount Hor to the Red Sea, they grew particularly impatient. They complained bitterly to Moses and accused him of bringing them into the desert to die. Their grumbling so displeased God that He brought them swift and severe punishment:

> Then the Lord sent venomous snakes among them; they bit the people and many Israelites died. The people came to Moses and said, "We sinned when we spoke against the Lord and against you. Pray that the Lord will take the snakes away from us." So Moses prayed for the people. (Numbers 21:6–7)

We can see from this passage that the Lord has little tolerance for the type of rebellious and arrogant behavior that brought forth this judgment. As the Scriptures say elsewhere, "For rebellion is as the sin of witchcraft, and stubbornness is as iniquity and idolatry" (1 Samuel 15:23 KJV).

But the Lord heeded the repentance of the people and answered Moses's prayer:

> The Lord said to Moses, "Make a snake and put it up on a pole; anyone who is bitten can look at it and live." So Moses made a bronze snake and put it up on a pole. Then when

anyone was bitten by a snake and looked at the
bronze snake, they lived. (Numbers 21:8–9)

The gospel of John makes clear the connection between this episode and the redemptive work of Jesus on the cross: "Just as Moses lifted up the snake in the wilderness, so the Son of Man must be lifted up, that everyone who believes may have eternal life in him" (John 3:14–15).

One detail of this Old Testament type of Christ is very intriguing. The snakebites are related to the power of sin and death over the nonbeliever. The pole clearly represents the cross on which Christ was crucified. But why, then, was Christ represented as a bronze snake? Snakes in the Scriptures normally represent the Devil or his demons.

The answer may have something to do with the fact that Jesus bore all of our sins and sicknesses as part of the atonement. As Isaiah 53:6 says, "We all, like sheep, have gone astray, each of us has turned to our own way; and the Lord has laid on him the iniquity of us all." The Bible further points out that in the process of bearing all of our sins and sicknesses, Christ actually became sin for us. He became a curse for our sake:

- God made him who had no sin to be sin for us, so that in him we might become the righteousness of God. (2 Corinthians 5:21)

- Christ redeemed us from the curse of the law by becoming a curse for us, for it is written [in Deuteronomy 21:23]: "Cursed is everyone who is hung on a pole." (Galatians 3:13)

Perhaps the worst part of the punishment Jesus suffered was not the beating, the scourging, and the humiliation He endured, but that awful moment on the cross when, as the end drew near, He sensed His Father's absence for the first time ever and exclaimed, "My God, my God, why have you forsaken me" (Matthew 27:46)? This must have been the moment when Jesus actually became a curse for us and when He most fully resembled that bronze snake.

The wilderness years contain other episodes that reveal additional facets of Christ's life and mission. For example, when Moses was speaking with God on one occasion, he asked the Lord to show him His glory. The Lord agreed, but on the condition that Moses must not see His face, "for no one may see me and live" (Exodus 33:20). The passage goes on:

> Then the Lord said, "There is a place near me where you may stand on a rock. When my glory passes by, I will put you in a cleft in the rock and cover you with my hand until I have passed by. Then I will remove my hand and you will see my back; but my face must not be seen." (Exodus 33:21–23)

This is the rock that was immortalized by the song "Rock of Ages." The rock had to be cleft, or split, in order for Moses to be protected while in the presence of God. Likewise, Jesus, our Rock of Ages, had to be broken on the cross in order to make a way for us to draw near to God. As the book of Hebrews points out, "We have confidence to enter the Most Holy Place by the blood of Jesus, by a new and living way opened for us through the curtain, that is, his body" (Hebrews 10:19–20).

But the Old Testament accounts of the wilderness years do not confine themselves to references to Jesus's suffering and death on the cross. They also contain symbols of the resurrection. On one particular occasion, the Lord used this kind of symbolism when He set aside Aaron and the house of Levi as priests. The Lord told Moses to collect twelve rods, one from each of the twelve tribes of Israel, and to write names upon the rods to identify them. Aaron's name was written upon the rod of the tribe of Levi. The Lord told Moses to leave the twelve rods in the tabernacle overnight. He also told him Aaron's rod would sprout. What happened next was quite phenomenal:

> The next day Moses entered the tent and saw that Aaron's staff, which represented the tribe of Levi, had not only sprouted but had budded, blossomed and produced almonds. Then Moses brought out all the staffs from the Lord's presence to all the Israelites. They looked at them, and each of the leaders took his own staff. (Numbers 17:8–9)

The Lord told Moses to store Aaron's rod in the tabernacle beside the ark as a future reminder to the Israelites so that they would not rebel.

From this account we can see several similarities between the resurrection of Jesus and the budding of Aaron's rod. Like Jesus, the rod had died, yet it lived again by the power of God. The evidence of the new life came in the morning, when Moses retrieved the rod from the tabernacle. Likewise, the evidence of Jesus's resurrection came in the morning, "early ... while it was still dark" (John 20:1). The rod was shown to the people publicly. Likewise, Jesus "appeared to more than five hundred of the brothers and sisters at the same time" after His resurrection (1 Corinthians 15:6). Finally, the rod was taken back into the tabernacle and kept in the presence of God beside the ark of the covenant. This compares with Jesus's ascending into heaven to be seated at the right hand of God. As usual, the physical events in the Old Testament foreshadowed much greater, supernatural events that were to happen later on. As Hebrews 9:24 points out, "Christ did not enter a sanctuary made with human hands that was only a copy of the true one; he entered heaven itself, now to appear for us in God's presence."

Moreover, Christ went to heaven not to serve as a reminder against rebellion, but to intercede for His people before the throne of God (Romans 8:34). So we can see that the parallel with Jesus is not perfect. But even in the contrasts we gain useful insights about how God operates: He frequently delivers more than He promises, and He saves the best for last.

The Lord continued to enliven the history of the Israelites with these prophetic portraits of Christ throughout Old Testament times. Another example of this symbolism is seen when the Israelites crossed the Jordan River on their way into the Promised Land.

The Lord parted the waters of the Jordan River when they crossed, just as He had parted the waters of the Red Sea forty years earlier when they left Egypt. After the Israelites walked across the Jordan on the river bottom, the Lord instructed them to take up twelve stones from the river bottom and to use them to construct a monument on the west bank "to be a memorial to the people of Israel forever" (Joshua 4:7). The Israelites did as the Lord instructed. These stones foreshadowed the Christian believers, who are described by the Scriptures as "living stones" (1 Peter 2:5). As the Scriptures further point out, God has "raised us up with Christ and seated us with him in the heavenly realms in Christ Jesus" (Ephesians 2:6).

The crossing of the Jordan River brought to a close a most remarkable chapter in the history of Israel. Throughout the Israelites' years in the wilderness, the Lord dealt with them in a series of fascinating incidents, some of which we can understand only in light of the New Testament. In retrospect, we can clearly see that the Israelites "drank from the spiritual rock that accompanied them, and that rock was Christ" (1 Corinthians 10:4).

CHAPTER 12
Decoding the Tabernacle and the Temple

During the time when the Israelites were wandering in the wilderness, a fundamental change took place in their relationship with God: He began to dwell among them. God had never dwelt among His people before. He had walked in the garden of Eden. He had walked with two outstanding men of faith, Enoch and Noah. But God had no dwelling place among any group of people as a whole until the construction of the tabernacle.

God assigned Moses the task of building the tabernacle during a forty-day visit to Mount Sinai: "Then have them make a sanctuary for me, and I will dwell among them. Make this tabernacle and all its furnishings exactly like the pattern I will show you" (Exodus 25:8–9). Note that the tabernacle was not designed by Moses, but by God Himself. As Hebrews 9:11 implies, it was meant to resemble "the greater and more perfect tabernacle that is not made with human hands, that is to say, is not a part of this creation." The tabernacle, therefore, was "a copy and shadow of what is in heaven" (Hebrews 8:5).

The Lord considered the tabernacle so important that He spent forty days with Moses carefully teaching him the details of its design, along with the design of the articles that were to go inside and the sacrifices that were to accompany its use. It was during this forty-day absence that the Israelites grew impatient and resorted to worshipping a golden calf.

The tabernacle was a portable structure the Israelites carried around with them during their wilderness journeys. It was set up inside a courtyard. It was thirty cubits long, ten cubits wide, and ten cubits high (a cubit is about a foot and a half). It consisted of two compartments: the first one was called the sanctuary, or the Holy Place, and the second one was called the Holy of Holies.

The sanctuary was twenty cubits by ten cubits. The priests could enter it from the courtyard, after first washing their hands and feet with water from a special basin set up near the entrance. The sanctuary contained a table, a candlestick, and specially made dishes and spoons. Bread was always kept on the table. The priests routinely entered the sanctuary in the course of performing their priestly duties of sacrifices and offerings.

The Holy of Holies was the innermost chamber of the tabernacle. It was a perfect cube, measuring ten cubits on all sides. It could be accessed only from the sanctuary, and it was separated from the sanctuary by a veil. The Holy of Holies contained the ark of the covenant, in which were stored the Ten Commandments and Aaron's rod that had budded. On top of the ark was the mercy seat, or cover, made of gold. On either end of this cover were two golden cherubim, angelic figures with wings extended over the mercy seat. The presence of the Lord dwelled over this mercy seat and between the two cherubim. Moses would meet with the Lord here to receive His commandments. Later, after the Israelites had entered the Promised Land, the high priest entered this chamber once a year, on the Day of Atonement, to make intercession on behalf of Israel.

Details of the construction of the tabernacle and of the instruments in it may be found in chapters 25 to 31 of the book of Exodus.

Some five hundred years after the construction of the tabernacle, the Israelites, led by King Solomon, built the temple, a permanent structure with the same basic form and function as the tabernacle, but with twice the dimensions. Although the tabernacle was an impressive structure in its own right, it could not compare with the temple. The tabernacle was a movable tent covered with badger skins. It had a sand floor. The temple, by contrast, was a carefully crafted, magnificent stone structure garnished with precious stones. Its walls were made of cedarwood overlaid with gold. The floor was also overlaid with gold. Details of the construction of the temple may be found in 1 Kings, chapters 5 through 8.

Both of these structures foreshadowed the person of Jesus Christ, in whom "all the fullness of the Deity lives in bodily form" (Colossians 2:9). Jesus compared Himself with the temple on at least two occasions. To the Jews who demanded a miraculous sign from Him to prove His authority, He replied, "Destroy this temple, and I will raise it again in three days" (John 2:19). The Jews were puzzled by this reply. "But the temple he had spoken of was his body" (John 2:21). On another occasion, Jesus said, "I tell you that something greater than the temple is here" (Matthew 12:6).

After Jesus rose from the dead and ascended into heaven, another basic change took place in the relationship of God with His people. There was no longer any need for a stone temple, because God had begun to dwell in them.

> Do you not know that your bodies are temples of the Holy Spirit, who is in you, whom you have received from God? You are not your own; you were bought at a price. Therefore honor God with your bodies. (1 Corinthians 6:19–20)

Therefore, in addition to foreshadowing Jesus Christ, the temple and the tabernacle also foreshadowed the time when God, through Jesus Christ and the Holy Spirit, would actually dwell in the hearts of His people. The apostle Paul, explaining the significance of this newly revealed "mystery" to the Colossians, described it as "Christ in you, the hope of glory" (Colossians 1:27).

The temple and the tabernacle also foreshadowed the collective body of God's people known as the body of Christ, or the church. Paul's letter to the Ephesians, another group of Gentiles, explains this concept:

> Consequently, you are no longer foreigners and strangers, but fellow citizens with God's people and also members of his household, built on the foundation of the apostles and prophets, with Christ Jesus himself as the chief cornerstone. In him the whole building is joined together and rises to become a holy temple in the Lord. And in him you too are being built together to become a dwelling in which God lives by his Spirit. (Ephesians 2:19–22)

It is noteworthy that this passage speaks of a building still under construction. Another scriptural passage elaborates on and reinforces this concept: "You also, like living stones, are being built into a spiritual house to be a holy priesthood, offering spiritual sacrifices acceptable to God through Jesus Christ" (1 Peter 2:5).

This passage supplies an additional piece of information: that the individual Christian believers are the key building blocks in the body of Christ, and they perform the same role in God's spiritual temple as the stones did in the physical temple that preceded it. But this spiritual temple is still under construction. It will not be complete until the individual "stones" are complete. This will not happen "until we all reach unity in the faith and in the knowledge of the Son of God and become mature, attaining to the whole measure of the fullness of Christ" (Ephesians 4:13). This process will be complete "when Christ appears, [when] we shall be like him, for we shall see him as he is" (1 John 3:2).

Meanwhile, as we await Christ's return, we dwell in temporary mortal bodies and together comprise the body of Christ on the earth, an imperfect, makeshift structure similar to the tabernacle. Like Abraham, we admit we are "foreigners and strangers on earth" (Hebrews 11:13). We dwell in imperfect, incomplete structures, knowing that "when completeness comes, what is in part disappears" (1 Corinthians 13:10).

In summary, the tabernacle foreshadowed the body of Christ on earth, while the temple foreshadowed the Church in its glorified, resurrected state after Christ's return. In addition, the tabernacle foreshadowed our mortal earthly bodies, while the temple foreshadowed our glorified resurrected bodies:

> For we know that if the earthly tent we live in is destroyed, we have a building from God, an eternal house in heaven, not built by human hands. Meanwhile we groan, longing to be clothed instead with our heavenly dwelling, because when we are clothed, we will not be found naked. For while we are in this tent, we groan and are burdened, because we do not wish to be unclothed but to be clothed instead with our heavenly dwelling, so that what is mortal may be swallowed up by life. (2 Corinthians 5:1–4)

We can gain a valuable insight into the Christian life and walk by following the reference to the living stones to its logical conclusion. The Scriptures contain a particularly intriguing detail about the construction of the temple. First Kings 6:7 tells us, "In building the temple, only blocks dressed at the quarry were used, and no hammer, chisel or any other iron tool was heard at the temple site while it was being built." In other words, the stones used in the temple were shaped and made ready at the quarry site before they were carried to the temple site to be installed in the temple. The Old Testament provides no clear explanation for this procedure, but the process certainly has meaning for us today. As God's "living stones," we too should seek to be shaped and made ready as much as possible while we are on the earth rather than wait passively for God to finish the job when we depart this life and go to heaven. The Scriptures clearly reinforce this concept by explaining that "we are God's handiwork, created in Christ Jesus to do good works, which God prepared in advance for us to do" (Ephesians 2:10), and urging that we "offer [our] bodies as a living sacrifice" (Romans 12:1). Jesus Himself reinforced this concept when He instructed us to pray, "Thy Kingdom come, Thy will be done, on earth as it is in heaven." When we pray this prayer with conviction, we can be assured that "the Kingdom of God has come near" (Mark 1:15). Thus, even though the ultimate heavenly temple is still under construction, there is work to be done in us and through us while we are still on the earth. God did not intend for the Christian life to consist of hanging on for dear life with white knuckles while waiting for the rapture.

What, then, are the steps we must go through to grow as Christian believers while we are here on earth?

The temple stones first had to be cut out of the earth and then brought to the surface. This is equivalent to salvation, which entails a person's being chosen as one of God's people and, therewith, being set aside from the rest of the world.

The temple stones then had to be shaped in the proper manner. Each stone had to have its rough edges chiseled off. It was then shaped and sanded to the proper dimensions and degree of smoothness. It had to be washed clean to be free from debris. Christian believers must undergo a similar process, but on the inside. This process can be rather painful at times, as the analogy implies.

The Lord uses certain tools in the performance of these processes. One of these tools is His Word. The Scriptures speak of "the washing with water through the word" (Ephesians 5:26). Jesus told His disciples, "You are already clean because of the word I have spoken to you" (John 15:3). But other tools have a degree of unpleasantness associated with them. The book of James speaks of one such tool:

> Consider it pure joy, my brothers and sisters, whenever you face trials of many kinds, because you know that the testing of your faith produces perseverance. Let perseverance finish its work so that you may be mature and complete, not lacking anything. (James 1:2–4)

From these passages, therefore, we can see that God uses the trials and difficulties of our lives to help us to grow into mature believers. These trials and difficulties may take innumerable forms, and they may be very uncomfortable at the time they are happening. But we may rest assured that "he who began a good work in [us] will carry it on to completion until the day of Christ Jesus" (Philippians 1:6).

Once a critical mass of mature Christian believers has been fitted together into a greater body, the result is gloriously greater than the sum of its parts. It becomes not just an organization that conducts weekly worship and fellowship, but a dwelling place for Jesus Christ on earth, and a powerful agent of renewal and redemption in the world.

CHAPTER 13
Decoding the Gospel of John

Why did God cause the gospel account to be handed down to us in four distinct books rather than in one consolidated account? We do not know for sure, but perhaps it was because the account needed to be told with four distinct approaches. Bible scholars have long noted that Matthew, Mark, Luke, and John each present the gospel in a different way.

The book of Matthew emphasizes Jesus Christ as God's chosen King. Hence, for example, the genealogy in Matthew 1 emphasizes Jesus's royal ancestry and traces Him back to Abraham. Mark presents Jesus as God's servant; hence, no genealogy is required. Luke presents Jesus as God's perfect Man. As in Matthew, there is a genealogy, but this time Jesus is traced all the way back to Adam, and the royal genealogy is not stressed. The gospel of John presents Jesus as God Himself; therefore, there is no need of a human genealogy since Jesus is presented as the eternal Son of God.

While each of the four gospels has its own individual traits, it is the gospel of John that stands most apart from the others. Some Bible scholars refer to the first three gospels as the "Synoptic Gospels" because of the similarity of their general order and content. These gospels speak of Jesus in human terms (king, servant, man), while John's gospel speaks of Jesus's divinity. This by itself obviously calls for a different approach by John, which probably accounts for much of the distinctive nature of John's gospel.

It is in the gospel of John that we find the famous "I am" statements of Jesus: "I am the bread of life" (John 6:35); "I am the light of the world" (8:12); I am the gate for the sheep" (10:7); etc. The phrase "I am" is the same phrase God gave to Moses as a means of identifying Him to the children of Israel (Exodus 3:14).

The gospel of John also makes extensive use of types in identifying Jesus. In it, we see Jesus identified as the true Lamb of God (John 1:29), and we see Him compared with Jacob's ladder (1:51), the temple (2:18–21), the brass serpent that Moses raised in the wilderness (3:14), Jacob's well (4:13–14), the manna (6:48–51), and the rock from which the living water flowed (7:37).

Another unique attribute of John's gospel is the way in which it is structured. Having just discussed the temple and the tabernacle in the previous chapter, we may now arrive at a better understanding of how John's gospel is organized. While the first three gospels are in fairly strict chronological order, this is not the case with the gospel of John. Rather, John's gospel is organized and laid out thematically.

Chapters 1 through 12 describe Jesus's public ministry. Jesus is shown attending a wedding, discussing theology with the Samaritan woman at the well, debating the Pharisees and Sadducees, healing the sick, raising the dead, and feeding and teaching the masses.

Chapters 13 through 16 portray Jesus in the private company of His disciples in the days leading up to His crucifixion. In chapter 13, Jesus is shown washing His disciples' feet. In chapters 14 through 16, Jesus discusses with the disciples some matters meant only for their ears, as the public was still unprepared to hear them. It was in this setting that Jesus taught His disciples about the Holy Spirit.

Chapters 17, 18, and 19 describe Jesus alone with the

Decoding Bible Messages

Father. Chapter 17 shows Jesus praying to the Father. In chapters 18 and 19, Jesus is arrested, abandoned by His disciples, and left to bear the punishment of the cross without any supportive human company.

Recall that the tabernacle consisted of a two-room building with a surrounding courtyard. All Israelites were admitted to the courtyard. This was the public part of the complex. The courtyard compares with the public part of Jesus's ministry, which is described in chapters 1 through 12 of John's gospel.

Only the priests were allowed in the Holy Place, or the sanctuary, the first room of the tabernacle itself. Chapters 13 through 16 of John correspond to this portion of the building. Chapter 13 describes a foot-washing ceremony, a purification ritual of the kind that would naturally precede entry into a holy place. This corresponds to the priests washing their hands and feet at the bronze basin near the entrance to the Holy Place before entering it. This is followed by Jesus's continuing to meet privately with His disciples in a manner resembling how the priests meet privately with God in the Holy Place.

Only the high priest could enter the Holy of Holies, and even then only once a year following a sacrifice. This corresponds to Jesus, our High Priest, alone with the Father and giving the sacrifice of Himself once and for all to cleanse us of our sins. This is described in John, chapters 17 through 19, which therefore correspond to the Holy of Holies. Note that Jesus's sacrifice is better than that of the high priest:

> He went through the greater and more perfect tabernacle that is not made with human hands, that is to say, is not a part of this creation. He did not enter by means of the blood of goats and calves; but he entered the Most Holy Place once for all by his own blood, thus obtaining eternal redemption. (Hebrews 9:11–12)

So we see that the gospel of John is organized along the lines of the tabernacle (see figure 4). Chapters 1 through 12 correspond to the outer courtyard, chapters 13 through 16 correspond to the sanctuary, and chapters 17 through 19 correspond to the Holy of Holies.

What of John, chapters 20 and 21? Chapter 21 is a sort of epilogue. In chapter 20, Jesus is restored to life and to His disciples, which makes this chapter stand apart from chapters 17 through 19. Nevertheless, I believe there is still a powerful connection between chapter 20 and the Holy of Holies, for in it the most sacred object in the entire tabernacle, the ark of the covenant, is decoded. John 20:11–12 describes what Mary Magdalene saw when she beheld Jesus's empty tomb: "As she wept, she bent over to look into the tomb and saw two angels in white, seated where Jesus's body had been, one at the head and the other at the foot" (John 20:11–12). Recall that the ark of the covenant was topped by a gold mercy seat, and on either end of the mercy seat were two golden angelic figures with their wings extended over it. Can there be any doubt that the golden angels at either end of the ark prefigured the two angels at either end of where Jesus's body had been laid? The ark of the covenant with the two angels on top and the empty space between them foreshadowed the empty tomb of Jesus Christ!

This is a fitting close for this brief study of the gospel of John. We do not know whether the writer John deliberately planned to structure his book like the tabernacle, or whether the Holy Spirit, without John's conscious knowledge, did it as John wrote. In any case, it is God-inspired, makes for a powerful and well-organized presentation, and further reinforces our conviction that Jesus is the central subject of the whole Bible.

FIGURE 4:
STRUCTURE OF THE GOSPEL OF JOHN

COURTYARD:
JOHN 1 - 12

<u>Jesus' public ministry</u>
- Attended a wedding
- Samaritan woman at the well
- Debated the Pharisees
- Healed the Sick
- Fed and taught the masses

HOLY PLACE:
JOHN 13 - 16

<u>Jesus with his disciples</u>
- Footwashing
- Taught about abiding in Christ
- Taught about the Holy Spirit

HOLIEST OF HOLIES:
JOHN 17 - 19

<u>Jesus Alone with the Father</u>
- Garden of Gethsemane
- Arrested and crucified

CHAPTER 14
Decoding the Life of David

When the Spirit of the Lord moves into a person's life, a challenge is often not far behind. Jesus's life is a prime example of this. As soon as He was baptized by John the Baptist and was filled with the Holy Spirit, He was driven into the wilderness for a time of fasting and communion with the Father. There, He endured forty days of hunger followed by a direct confrontation with Satan. Satan tried to get Jesus to abuse His powers and to worship him, but he failed miserably in the attempt, as Jesus sent Satan away with three quotes from the book of Deuteronomy. Thereafter, Jesus inflicted one defeat after another upon Satan and his kingdom.

About a thousand years earlier, a man named David also had a divine anointing followed by a confrontation with the enemy.

David's life started out inconspicuously in a little town called Bethlehem (1 Samuel 16:1–13), also the birthplace of the Jewish Messiah a thousand years later. He worked in obscurity as a shepherd until the prophet Samuel was sent by God to anoint the man who would be the next king of Israel. Having been told the next king would be one of the sons of Jesse, Samuel went directly to Jesse and explained his mission. Jesse brought out his sons one by one, but there was no future king found among them. Finally, when all other possibilities had been exhausted, Jesse brought forth his youngest son, David, who had been in the pasture tending sheep. What happened next must have been the outcome least expected by the people assembled there:

> Then the Lord said, "Rise and anoint him; this is the one." So Samuel took the horn of oil and anointed him in the presence of his brothers, and from that day on the Spirit of the Lord came powerfully upon David. (1 Samuel 16:12–13)

The surprise of David's family must have been similar to that displayed by the family and friends of Jesus when He preached and taught in His own hometown: "'Isn't this the carpenter? Isn't this Mary's son and the brother of James, Joseph, Judas and Simon? Aren't his sisters here with us?' And they took offense at him" (Mark 6:3).

Things did not change very much in Israel over the course of a thousand years in at least one key respect: the Israelites tended to "look at the outward appearance" (1 Samuel 16:7) when considering who was worthy to be their leader, and were reluctant to recognize a God-anointed leader who did not burst upon the scene in splendor and majesty. Such are the differences between our way and God's way.

David's characteristics as a shepherd prefigured Jesus's own identity as the "good shepherd" (John 10:11). There are at least two indications of this. The first indication is David's tenacious protection of his sheep, which he himself described to Saul:

> Your servant has been keeping his father's sheep. When a lion or a bear came and carried off a sheep from the flock, I went after it, struck it and rescued the sheep from its mouth.

> When it turned on me, I seized it by its hair, struck it and killed it. (1 Samuel 17:34–35)

Jesus taught a lesson on this very theme when He said, "If a man owns a hundred sheep, and one of them wanders away, will he not leave the ninety-nine on the hills and go to look for the one that wandered off" (Matthew 18:12)? David did that very thing whenever a sheep under his care encountered danger. This must have been one of the qualities God was looking for in Israel's next king. As Jesus said in a parable, "Because you have been trustworthy in a very small matter, take charge of ten cities" (Luke 19:17).

Another prophetic portrait of Jesus is found in David's provision for his sheep when he was separated from them. When David was sent by his father to take supplies to his brothers in Saul's army, he "left the flock in the care of a shepherd" (1 Samuel 17:20). Similarly, when it was time for Jesus to depart from His earthly flock, He promised His disciples, "I will ask the Father, and he will give you another advocate," the Holy Spirit (John 14:16). Finally, when Jesus was about to ascend into heaven, He entrusted the care of the church to Peter and the other apostles: "Take care of my sheep," He told Peter (John 21:16).

Just as David may be recognized as a type of Jesus Christ, so also may Goliath be recognized as a type of Satan. Goliath was a Philistine giant who came forward to confront the Israelites in the Valley of Elah, where the two armies were facing one another. He issued a challenge to the Israelites:

> "Choose a man and have him come down to me. If he is able to fight and kill me, we will become your subjects; but if I overcome him and kill him, you will become our subjects and serve us." ... For forty days the Philistine came

forward every morning and evening and took his stand. (1 Samuel 17:8–9, 16)

This persistent taunt reminds us of the New Testament description of Satan as "a roaring lion looking for someone to devour" (1 Peter 5:8). Notice also that the Israelites endured this challenge for forty days, the same amount of time Jesus spent fasting in the wilderness after His baptism (Matthew 4:2).

In each case, the forty-day challenge began very soon after God anointed the individual with the Holy Spirit. Each challenge was climaxed by a direct, head-to-head confrontation with the enemy.

David persuaded Saul to allow him to fight Goliath. After Saul agreed, he outfitted David with his armor and weapons. However, David was unaccustomed to them and decided instead to utilize the tools of his shepherding trade. First Samuel 17:40 tells us that David "chose five smooth stones from the stream, put them in the pouch of his shepherd's bag and, with his sling in his hand, approached the Philistine."

By his rejection of traditional, worldly weapons, the Holy Spirit through David illustrated the New Testament truth that "the weapons of our warfare are not carnal but mighty in God for pulling down strongholds" (2 Corinthians 10:4 NKJV).

When the time for combat had come, Goliath began to move toward David for the attack. Almost everyone knows what David did next: "Reaching into his bag and taking out a stone, he slung it and struck the Philistine on the forehead. The stone sank into his forehead, and he fell facedown on the ground" (1 Samuel 17:49).

David then took Goliath's *own* sword from its sheath and cut off the Philistine giant's head.

When Jesus faced the Devil in the wilderness, He armed Himself with the Word of God. In Jesus's day, the Scriptures consisted of what we know today as the Old Testament. The Jews especially prized the five books of Moses called the

Pentateuch, or the Torah. We may be sure that Jesus carried around the contents of these five books in His mind, just as David carried the five stones in his shepherd's bag. When the Devil made his move to attack Jesus with his temptations, Jesus was ready. He selected one of the five books, the book of Deuteronomy, and hurled it at the Devil's face:

- Man shall not live on bread alone, but on every word that comes from the mouth of God. (Matthew 4:4, quoted from Deuteronomy 8:3)

- Do not put the Lord your God to the test. (Matthew 4:7, quoted from Deuteronomy 6:16)

- Worship the Lord your God, and serve him only. (Matthew 4:10, quoted from Deuteronomy 6:13)

The Devil, once he was defeated, fled, unable to deter God's appointed Messiah from His mission. Jesus then proceeded to fulfill His mission on the cross, where, through death, *Satan's own weapon* (Hebrews 2:14), Jesus delivered the final blow to Satan that would guarantee his defeat for all ages. It is only a matter of time before the full extent of Satan's defeat will be realized. Then the earliest prophecy of Satan's destruction in the book of Genesis will come true: "He [the Messiah] will crush your [Satan's] head" (Genesis 3:15).

David's subsequent career continued to reflect his role as a deliverer of his people. He was successful in all of his campaigns against Israel's enemies. In fact, he was so successful that King Saul began to feel threatened by him. Saul began to plot his death. This reaction was similar to the reaction of Israel's religious leaders when Jesus's fame and popularity grew. On a number of occasions, David had to flee in order to slip out of Saul's grasp, just as Jesus had to slip through the crowd on several occasions to escape a premature death or arrest. But David never retaliated against Saul, nor did he take up the sword against any of his fellow Israelites. Jesus likewise did not retaliate against the people who were out to kill Him, and He forbade His disciples to take up the sword in His defense when His arrest finally came (Matthew 26:52).

On one occasion, while fleeing from Saul, David took refuge in a cave called Adullam. While he was there, "All those who were in distress or in debt or discontented gathered around him, and he became their commander. About four hundred men were with him" (1 Samuel 22:2). This foreshadowed Jesus's practice of recruiting ordinary people of His day to be His disciples. Jesus also (in the parable of the wedding banquet) had His servants round up wedding guests from "the street corners ... the bad as well as the good" (Matthew 22:9–10).

David ultimately did become king of Israel, just as Jesus will one day physically return to take His rightful place on the throne of the world.

Of course, the type breaks down in a number of key aspects. David was a mere human being who ruled temporarily and had sin in his life. Jesus, the Son of God, is without sin, and His kingdom is eternal. David, unlike Jesus, never had to lay down his life before being made king, though he had a number of narrow escapes. But these contrasts only serve to accentuate the glory of Jesus, our true deliverer for all times.

CHAPTER 15
Decoding the Lives of the Heroes of the Faith

We have seen how some of the major characters of the Old Testament led lives that paralleled the life of Jesus in some remarkable ways. With Isaac, we found parallels occurring in the events surrounding his birth and his near sacrifice. With Moses, the parallels occurred at several different times of his life, but most notably in the offices he held (shepherd, priest, deliverer, judge, ruler, etc.). David's life also paralleled Jesus's life on several occasions, especially at the time of his anointing and the confrontation with the enemy that followed it. Joseph's entire life was virtually one long, encoded biography of Jesus.

These individuals were not isolated examples but merely the most striking of a whole host of lives that in some way foreshadowed the Jewish Messiah. It can also be said that each of the major dimensions of Jesus's life and ministry was prophetically portrayed by at least one Old Testament character, and often multiple characters.

The teachings and warnings of Jesus aroused great ire among the religious establishment of His day. But such teachings and warnings were not at all without precedent. Jesus was often simply repeating what the prophets had said hundreds of years before. These prophets had aroused strong feelings in their day because of their repeated calls for national repentance, but they were revered by the Israelites in Jesus's time. Jesus Himself recognized this irony and pointed it out on more than one occasion. On one such occasion, Jesus had this to say to the Pharisees while He was visiting the temple grounds:

> I am sending you prophets and sages and teachers. Some of them you will kill and crucify; others you will flog in your synagogues and pursue from town to town. And so upon you will come all the righteous blood that has been shed on earth, from the blood of righteous Abel to the blood of Zechariah son of Berekiah, whom you murdered between the temple and the altar. (Matthew 23:34–35)

Jesus went on to contribute His own righteous blood, just as had those who had come before Him. The hearts and minds of the Pharisees proved impervious to the lessons of history.

The miracles of Jesus stirred great wonder, but some of them had been done before. The lives of Elijah and Elisha as described in 1 and 2 Kings provide some examples.

Jesus miraculously fed a multitude of people with a small quantity of food (Matthew 15:32–38). Elijah miraculously fed himself, along with a widow from Sidon and her son, for an extended period of time from jars containing small quantities of flour and oil (1 Kings 17:7–16). When the widow's son fell ill and died, Elijah appealed to the Lord and the child was raised from the dead (1 Kings 17:17–24). Jesus also raised a widow's son from the dead (Luke 7:11–15).

Elijah, like Jesus, traveled forty days and forty nights in the wilderness and was fed by an angel (1 Kings 19 and Matthew 4:1–11). Both Elijah and Jesus performed miraculous feats with water: Jesus calmed the storm on the Sea of Galilee

(Mark 4:39), and Elijah parted the Jordan River just before he was taken up into heaven (2 Kings 2:8).

This ascension into heaven also foreshadows Jesus's ascension (Acts 1:9). There is still one other case of such an ascension: that of Enoch (Genesis 5:24). Both of these foreshadow not only Jesus's ascension, but also that of the entire church sometime in the future, at a time of the Father's own choosing (1 Thessalonians 4:14–17).

Elisha received a double portion of Elijah's anointing and continued in the tradition of his mentor. Elisha parted the Jordan River as he was returning from the west bank, where Elijah had been taken up into heaven (2 Kings 2:14). He also raised a child from the dead (2 Kings 4:32–37). He subsequently healed a case of leprosy in Naaman the Syrian general (2 Kings 5), a feat that was not to be repeated until the coming of Jesus.

In addition to featuring some of the same miracles Jesus performed, the accounts of the Old Testament heroes of the faith also contain veiled references to Jesus's sacrificial death and resurrection. We have already studied some of these references, but there are many more. The case of the prophet Jonah is a memorable example.

Jonah was instructed by God to preach to the people of Nineveh, but he tried to flee instead of obeying the Lord's command. After Jonah boarded a ship at Joppa and set sail for Tarshish, the Lord sent a great storm to batter the ship because of Jonah's disobedience. Jonah knew he was to blame for the storm, so he had himself thrown overboard in order to save the lives of his shipmates (Jonah 1). The Lord commanded a great fish to swallow Jonah, after which time Jonah spent three days and three nights in the belly of the fish before being vomited up onto dry land (Jonah 2).

Jesus referred to this episode in His teachings as a prophetic portrait of His own death and resurrection:

> A wicked and adulterous generation asks for a sign! But none will be given it except the sign of the prophet Jonah. For as Jonah was three days and three nights in the belly of a huge fish, so the Son of Man will be three days and three nights in the heart of the earth. The men of Nineveh will stand up at the judgment with this generation and condemn it; for they repented at the preaching of Jonah, and now something greater than Jonah is here. (Matthew 12:39–41)

Jesus pointed out that He was greater than Jonah because He willingly went on His mission whereas Jonah had to be forced into obedience. Thus, the familiar pattern repeats itself: the precision of the type is limited by the imperfections of the person in whose life the type is found.

Still another example of Christ's death and resurrection foreshadowed is Daniel, who served King Darius of Babylon during the exile. Daniel 6 contains the full account. Like Christ, Daniel was a blameless man who was falsely accused. The official in charge sought to have him released, but in the end the sentence had to be carried out. Daniel was thrown into a den of lions, representing near-certain death, and a stone was rolled over the opening. The next morning, at dawn's first light, the king hurried to the "tomb" to check on Daniel, and found he had survived unharmed. Daniel was immediately released from the den, thus foreshadowing Christ's release from the tomb.

Daniel's friends and fellow exiles, Shadrach, Meshach, and Abednego, also experienced a miraculous deliverance (Daniel 3). In this instance, it appears that their deliverance foreshadowed our rescue from judgment and the fires of hell as a result of our trust in Jesus Christ, who was actually seen with the three exiles in the midst of the fiery furnace.

Decoding Bible Messages

And so it goes for the other, major Old Testament characters. In the lives of the judges such as Joshua, Gideon, and Samson, we see foreshadowed the victory won by Jesus over our enemies in the spiritual realm. In Samson's case, his final victory came at the cost of his own life. In the careers of Solomon and Nehemiah, we see foreshadowed the work of Jesus in building His church, which the Bible calls "a holy temple in the Lord" (Ephesians 2:21). In the Levitical priesthood, we see foreshadowed the church itself, whose members "will be priests of God and of Christ"—and these "will reign with him for a thousand years" (Revelation 20:6). In the glorious reign of King Solomon, we are allowed to catch a glimpse of the thousand-year reign of Christ on earth during the millennium.

Though all of these dimensions of Jesus's life (miracles, deliverance, resurrection, etc.) have their Old Testament counterparts, never before had all of these elements been rolled up so completely into the life of one individual. Like the spokes of a wheel pointing to a central hub, these types overwhelmingly point to the life and work of Jesus Christ. Jesus is the ultimate object of all of the prophetic signs that came before Him.

CHAPTER 16
Decoding the Recurring Symbols of the Bible

Ordinary things often take on special meaning in the Scriptures.

Throughout the Scriptures, for example, yeast almost always represents sin. Salt, on the other hand, usually represents integrity. Garments were often used to foreshadow being clothed with the righteousness of Christ. The Holy Spirit had many symbols foreshadowing Him, including the dove, oil, clouds, fire, and water. Stones could be used to represent the twelve tribes of Israel or to foreshadow the individual Christian believers.

Jesus was foreshadowed by a multitude of characters, events, and elements of Hebrew culture. The occupation of shepherd, for instance, foreshadowed Jesus's relationship to the church. Many well-known characters of the Old Testament were shepherds, including Abel, Jacob, Joseph, Moses, and David. The Twenty-third Psalm reads, "The Lord is my shepherd." As we have seen, Jesus was also symbolically represented by Noah's ark, the ram that took Isaac's place, the Passover lamb, the rock that gave forth water, Aaron's rod that budded, the tabernacle, the temple, and many other things.

In this chapter, and in the one to follow, I will attempt to describe a few more symbols not dealt with previously. The reader should understand these are only thumbnail sketches of representative examples. It is not the mission of this book to offer a comprehensive treatment of this vast subject.

Yeast is one of the symbols of the Bible that merits some additional attention. Since the Lord used yeast as a symbol of sin, He ordered the Israelites to use unleavened bread for most of their feasts and offerings. Clearly, the bread that represented Christ's body in the Passover ceremony had to be unleavened. In addition, every Jewish household had to be purged of all yeast before the Passover. This cleansing of the Jewish home represented a cleansing from sin.

Such sin could include accepting false teachings as well as performing specific acts of wrongdoing. When Jesus warned His disciples about the wrong teachings of the religious establishment, He said, "Be on your guard against the yeast of the Pharisees and Sadducees" (Matthew 16:11).

The Bible further explains the symbolism behind yeast in Paul's first letter to the Corinthians. In this letter we find a solemn warning about the insidious nature of sin. Sin, like yeast, has a tendency to spread like an infection through the life of an individual or a body of believers if left unchecked. This was the danger the Corinthian believers were facing because of their toleration of a particularly grievous sin in their midst (1 Corinthians 5:1–2). Paul was alarmed by this trend, so he sternly warned the Corinthians:

> Your boasting is not good. Don't you know that a little yeast leavens the whole batch of dough? Get rid of the old yeast, so that you may be a new unleavened batch—as you really are. For Christ, our Passover lamb, has been sacrificed. Therefore let us keep the Festival, not with the old bread leavened with malice and wickedness, but with the unleavened bread of sincerity and truth. (1 Corinthians 5:6–8)

Another frequently used symbol in the Bible is salt. Unlike yeast, salt is a preservative and is used to represent honesty, sincerity, and truth.

According to K. C. Pillai in chapter 2 of *Light through an Eastern Window,* Middle Eastern culture has long included a ritual known as the covenant of salt. A means of sealing an agreement, it consists of eating a portion of salt with one's partner. Agreements made in this fashion are considered ironclad and inviolable.

References to this type of covenant appear in the Scriptures in several places. For example, God had a covenant of salt with the Levites:

> Whatever is set aside from the holy offerings the Israelites present to the Lord I give to you and your sons and daughters as your perpetual share. It is an everlasting covenant of salt before the Lord for both you and your offspring. (Numbers 18:19)

The Lord also had a covenant of salt with the entire nation of Israel. The Lord instructed the Israelites to season all of their grain offerings with salt (Leviticus 2:13). Since this type of agreement cannot ever be violated, one can argue that the Lord still has a valid covenant with the Jewish people to this day, even though the new covenant of Jesus Christ is superior to the old covenant.

The New Testament also contains references to salt. For example, Jesus called His disciples "the salt of the earth" (Matthew 5:13), cautioning them against losing their saltiness.

This has given rise to questions about how salt could lose its saltiness. According to *Light through an Eastern Window,* chapter 2, Middle Easterners in ancient times would keep salt in large stone vessels in the kitchen. The salt was not table salt as we know it today, but rock salt containing impurities.

After the kitchen floor was washed repeatedly, water often seeped into the stone vessels and dissolved the salt near the bottom, leaving a saltlike residue that had no saltiness. This residue was useless and was thrown out after the good salt above it had been used up.

Judas's betrayal of Jesus was made especially serious by these Middle Eastern customs. When Jesus was with His disciples at the Last Supper, He identified His betrayer as the one who was sharing His bowl. The food in the bowl almost certainly contained some salt, given salt's widespread use as a preservative. This sharing gave Judas a special covenant with Jesus and made his betrayal particularly heinous.

Physical objects were not the only things in the Scriptures with symbolic significance. Some of the actions and processes involved in preparing offerings also had deeper meanings. In many of the Israelite ceremonies, there were instructions for offerings to be pierced and/or parted in pieces, and for blood to be poured out. The brass serpent in the wilderness was lifted upon a pole, and the rock was struck in order to obtain water. These processes all symbolize things that happened to Jesus at the time of His crucifixion.

Many substances were to be mashed or beaten. The grain offering is a good example. It did not involve animals but, instead, used grain ground into fine flour that was then baked without yeast. Incense and oil were added to it (Leviticus 2:14–15). A portion of it was burned on the altar, and the remainder belonged to the priests. The crushing of the grain foreshadowed the bruising and breaking of Jesus's body on the cross. The oil represents the Holy Spirit, who descended upon Jesus and anointed Him when He was baptized. The incense represents the spices with which Jesus's body was embalmed when He was buried in the tomb.

The act of piercing, and the tools associated with it, are another interesting area of study. Nails or goads are used symbolically in several places in the Bible. One of these passages is

Ecclesiastes 12:11: "The words of the wise are like goads, their collected sayings like firmly embedded nails—given by one shepherd." As we now know, the "one shepherd" in this Old Testament prophecy is Jesus Himself. The words of the wise given by this Good Shepherd, then, must be the Word of God.

A more familiar passage in the New Testament has similar things to say about the Word of God: "For the word of God is alive and active. Sharper than any double-edged sword, it penetrates even to dividing soul and spirit, joints and marrow; it judges the thoughts and attitudes of the heart" (Hebrews 4:12). The Word of God, mixed with the power of the Holy Spirit, has demonstrated its power to change people's hearts time and again. Scripture records numerous instances of miraculous changes brought about by the piercing effects of inspired words spoken by Spirit-filled believers. For example, when the disciples of Jesus were first filled with the Holy Spirit and began to speak in tongues, Peter confronted a crowd of amazed Jewish pilgrims and preached a spontaneous but inspired sermon that resulted in three thousand souls coming to Christ. The book of Acts is vivid in its description of the effect of Peter's words on the crowd: "When the people heard this, they were cut to the heart and said to Peter and the other apostles, 'Brothers, what shall we do'" (Acts 2:37)?

The Bible elsewhere states that such words have the power to lay bare the secrets of a person's heart (1 Corinthians 14:25). Such power, of course, is dependent on the activity of the Holy Spirit, for "no one can say, 'Jesus is Lord,' except by the Holy Spirit" (1 Corinthians 12:3). The Scriptures also state that the Holy Spirit "will reprove the world of sin, and of righteousness, and of judgment" (John 16:8 KJV). In order to have such a penetrating effect on a person's heart, the Holy Spirit uses a weapon, "the sword of the Spirit, which is the word of God" (Ephesians 6:17). The term "Word of God" in the Greek text means any messages or utterances inspired by God, not just the Scriptures.

The foregoing information can now be used to help decode a curious phrase in some versions of the Bible regarding Saul's conversion on the road to Damascus:

> As he journeyed he came near Damascus, and suddenly a light shone around him from heaven. Then he fell to the ground, and heard a voice saying to him, "Saul, Saul, why are you persecuting Me?" And he said, "Who are You, Lord?" Then the Lord said, "I am Jesus, whom you are persecuting. It is hard for you to kick against the goads." (Acts 9:3–5 NKJV)

According to *Light through an Eastern Window*, chapter 9, the last phrase of the above quotation refers to an old method of controlling an ox while plowing a field. The plowman would prick the ox with a goad to keep it in the furrow. A rebellious ox may kick at the plowman, but the clever plowman would hold the goad so that the ox would kick into it.

Jesus had a plan for Saul's life and was probably trying to reach Saul well before his conversion. Saul resisted fiercely, and actually began to persecute people for their Christian faith. But the more Saul resisted, the closer the Lord closed in on him until that final confrontation on the Damascus road. It is likely that the martyrdom of Stephen played an important role in weakening Saul's resistance. The last thing Saul saw and heard before Stephen died was a face like that of an angel and a prayer for Saul's forgiveness. This must have made quite an impression on him. Thus, Saul's savage kick at Jesus was met with a powerful prick to Saul's conscience.

This episode also shows the miraculous effect of a Christian's intercessory prayer. If Stephen had not prayed for Saul's forgiveness in his dying breath, then the church may never have acquired Saul, also known as Paul, the author of thirteen of the twenty-seven books of the New Testament.

CHAPTER 17
Decoding the Signs of God's Presence

Throughout history, the Lord has often used ordinary things as signals of His presence in our midst.

We have already seen that the Lord went ahead of the Israelites in a pillar of cloud by day and in a pillar of fire by night while He was guiding them through the wilderness. As noted earlier, this foreshadowed the day-to-day guidance Christians now receive from the Holy Spirit.

As we delve more deeply into the Scriptures, we see that a pattern emerges: the presence of the Lord is very often heralded by clouds. This common denominator stretches across both the Old and the New Testaments, allowing us to recognize a startling degree of consistency in passages that would otherwise appear to be unrelated.

When Moses went up to Mount Sinai to receive the Ten Commandments and to obtain instructions for building the tabernacle, the cloud was there with him (Exodus 24:15–18). The cloud was also present at the tabernacle when Moses finished building it (Exodus 40:33–38). The cloud stayed with the Israelites throughout their wilderness travels (Exodus 13:22).

The Lord finally took the cloud away when the Israelites finished their wilderness journeys and entered the Promised Land. But the cloud was to make several return visits. One such return visit happened several hundred years later, on the occasion of the completion of the temple:

> When the priests withdrew from the Holy Place, the cloud filled the temple of the Lord. And the priests could not perform their service because of the cloud, for the glory of the Lord filled his temple. Then Solomon said, "The Lord has said that he would dwell in a dark cloud; I have indeed built a magnificent temple for you, a place for you to dwell forever." (1 Kings 8:10–13)

The cloud continued to make return visits during New Testament times. One such return visit happened when Jesus was transfigured in the presence of some of His disciples:

> A bright cloud covered them, and a voice from the cloud said, "This is my Son, whom I love; with him I am well pleased. Listen to him!" When the disciples heard this, they fell face-down to the ground, terrified. But Jesus came and touched them. "Get up," he said. "Don't be afraid." (Matthew 17:5–7)

The cloud seemed to have a powerful effect on the people present. They were often so overwhelmed by the presence of God that they were unable to remain standing. The apostle Paul described this effect as he recounted his conversion experience to King Agrippa: "About noon, King Agrippa, as I was on the road, I saw a light from heaven, brighter than the sun, blazing around me and my companions. We all fell to the ground" (Acts 26:13–14).

Saul's description of his encounter with God in the form of a blinding light blazing around him looks very similar to the experience of Jesus's disciples at the transfiguration. Evidently, there is real, physical energy accompanying the presence of God that has an impact on the normal functioning of the human body.

It is interesting to note that as the disciples watched Jesus ascend into heaven, "a cloud hid him from their sight" (Acts 1:9). Immediately afterward, two angels promised the disciples that one day Jesus would return "in the same way you have seen him go into heaven" (Acts 1:11). Elsewhere, we are told that when Christ returns for His church, we will be "caught up ... in the clouds to meet the Lord in the air" (1 Thessalonians 4:17). So clouds will accompany Christ's return.

The Bible contains many other indicators of God's presence. The dove was used as such an indicator when Jesus was baptized in the Jordan River (Matthew 3:16–17). Oil was another indicator of God's presence. The Twenty-third Psalm foreshadowed the anointing of the Holy Spirit when the psalmist wrote, "You anoint my head with oil" (verse 5). The book of James prescribes the anointing of the sick with oil in order to apply the Holy Spirit's power to heal illness:

> Is anyone among you sick? Let them call the elders of the church to pray over them and anoint them with oil in the name of the Lord. And the prayer offered in faith will make the sick person well; the Lord will raise him up. If they have sinned, they will be forgiven. (James 5:14–15)

Another symbol of the power and presence of the Holy Spirit is the wind. This is reflected by the fact that both the Greek and Hebrew words for "spirit" also mean "wind." When Jesus described the Holy Spirit's activity to Nicodemus, He used the wind to illustrate His point: "The wind blows wherever it pleases. You hear its sound, but you cannot tell where it comes from or where it is going. So it is with everyone born of the Spirit" (John 3:8).

Jesus's description was borne out and reinforced by the manner in which the disciples received the Holy Spirit on the day of Pentecost:

> When the day of Pentecost came, they were all together in one place. Suddenly a sound like the blowing of a violent wind came from heaven and filled the whole house where they were sitting. They saw what seemed to be tongues of fire that separated and came to rest on each of them. All of them were filled with the Holy Spirit and began to speak in other tongues as the Spirit enabled them. (Acts 2:1–4)

This passage contains another emblem of the Holy Spirit, for we see that fire is also used as a symbol of the Holy Spirit's presence.

Fire is used as such a symbol in other Scripture passages as well. When Moses was called up to Mount Sinai, the Lord's presence took on the appearance of fire (Exodus 24:17). John the Baptist said Jesus would baptize His disciples "with the Holy Spirit and fire" (Matthew 3:11). When God made a covenant with Abraham and accepted his offering of sacrificed animals, we are told that "a smoking firepot with a blazing torch appeared and passed between the pieces" (Genesis 15:17).

The understanding gained from these passages may be used to interpret other passages in which the symbolism is less clear and is more subject to interpretation. A prime example of this is one of the military battles waged by the Israelites under the leadership of Gideon. When the Israelites were threatened by the forces of Midian, Gideon raised an army of thirty-two thousand men to defend Israel. The Lord winnowed this army down to three hundred men before

Decoding Bible Messages

allowing Gideon to attack. When Gideon prepared his attack, he directed his troops to carry trumpets, and jars containing torches, with them. Then, after surrounding the Midianites in the middle of the night,

> They blew their trumpets and broke the jars that were in their hands. ... While each man held his position around the camp, all the Midianites ran, crying out as they fled. ... [T]he Lord caused the men throughout the camp to turn on each other with their swords. (Judges 7:19, 21–22)

The Midianites fled in panic, with the victorious Israelites in hot pursuit.

This is a splendid representation of what God can do through Christian believers today. The jars, or earthen vessels, may be taken to represent our earthly bodies. The torches within the jars, therefore, represent the indwelling Holy Spirit. As we allow ourselves to be broken by God, thus dying to self, the power of the Holy Spirit is made manifest in our lives. We may then be used by God to perform great works beyond our human capabilities. As the Lord said to Paul, "My power is made perfect in weakness" (2 Corinthians 12:9).

This episode therefore foreshadowed the day when we would be able to become portable containers of God's Holy Spirit, carrying around a portion of God's light for all to see. As Jesus told His disciples, "Let your light shine before men, that they may see your good deeds and praise your Father in heaven" (Matthew 5:16).

CHAPTER 18
Decoding the Names of God

Thousands of years ago in the deserts of Midian on a mountain called Horeb, an eighty-year-old shepherd named Moses suddenly found himself in the presence of the living God. The time had come to bring the Israelites out of Egypt, and Moses was the one whom God had selected to lead them out. As the startled Moses began to grasp the enormity of what God was asking him to do, some questions naturally began to form in his mind. One question was a very practical one: "Suppose I go to the Israelites and say to them, 'The God of your fathers has sent me to you,' and they ask me, 'What is his name?' Then what shall I tell them" (Exodus 3:13)? The Lord gave Moses a most curious and intriguing reply: "I Am Who I Am. This is what you are to say to the Israelites: 'I Am has sent me to you'" (Exodus 3:14).

Thus did God provide a proper name for Himself for the first time in His dealings with humanity. This name, rendered Yhwh or Yahweh when transliterated from the Hebrew, is the root from which the word *Jehovah* is derived.

A merely superficial study of the Bible is enough to show that the Lord did not reveal Himself to humanity all at once. Instead, He did so gradually, over a period of many years. When viewed from this perspective, the name that God revealed to Moses takes on the character of a "fill-in-the-blank," or "I Am _____." Over the ensuing years, the

Lord proceeded to fill in this blank with some important information about Himself.

For example, when the Lord allowed Moses to turn the bitter waters of Marah into sweet waters, He gave him a message for the Israelites:

> If you listen carefully to the Lord your God and do what is right in his eyes, if you pay attention to his commands and keep all his decrees, I will not bring on you any of the diseases I brought on the Egyptians, for I am the Lord who heals you. (Exodus 15:26)

Thus, the Lord was no longer merely "I AM _____," but "I AM the LORD who heals you." The Lord filled in the blank in many other ways over the years. He revealed Himself as the provider (Genesis 22:14), the "Banner" (Exodus 17:15), "the Lord who makes you holy" (Exodus 31:13), and "the-Lord-is-peace" (Judges 6:24 NKJV). He also revealed Himself as "the Lord of Hosts" (1 Samuel 1:3 KJV), "the Lord Our Righteous Savior" (Jeremiah 23:6), "the Lord Most High" (Psalm 7:17), and "my shepherd" (Psalm 23:1).

These descriptive names significantly enriched the Israelites' understanding of the nature and character of God, and thereby enriched our understanding as well.

When Jesus finally came and walked the earth, teaching the multitudes and calling forth disciples, He was God in human flesh (John 1:14).

Jesus represented a quantum leap in God's revelation of Himself to humankind. He also showed by His life and His works how a true man or woman of God should live. During His teachings, He made a number of startling statements about Himself that all began with "I am." Thus, Jesus continued to fill in the blank God had given to Moses some fifteen hundred years earlier. A list of these statements follows:

- John 6:35: "I am the bread of life."
- John 8:12: "I am the light of the world."
- John 10:7: "I am the gate for the sheep."
- John 10:11: "I am the good shepherd."
- John 11:25: "I am the resurrection and the life."
- John 14:6: "I am the way and the truth and the life."
- John 15:1: "I am the true vine."

Jesus made perhaps His most startling statement of all at the conclusion of a long discussion with a hostile group of Pharisees at the temple. After the Pharisees had challenged Jesus's credentials, including raising the issue of whether His coming had been foreseen by Abraham, Jesus replied, "Very truly I tell you ... before Abraham was born, I am" (John 8:58)! In making this statement, Jesus was using the same term God had used in identifying Himself to Moses. The meaning was unmistakable: Jesus was equating Himself with God. This message was not lost on the angry Pharisees, who reacted by reaching for stones to throw at Him. Of course, this was not the time or the appointed manner of Jesus's death, so He slipped away from them and left the temple.

As befits the progressive nature of God's revelation of Himself, Jesus gave us a more intimate and personal portrait of God through these statements than God had given the Israelites. Most of the descriptive names the Lord gave to the Israelites spoke of Him in terms of what He *does* for His people: heal them, sanctify them, send peace, provide for them, and act as shepherd, banner, guide, etc. However, the descriptive names used by Jesus speak of Him in terms of who He *is*. When Jesus said, "I am the resurrection and the life," He did not mean He has control over life; rather, He meant that He *is* life. Similarly, He does not merely provide the bread of life; He *is* the Bread of Life. He does not merely provide the light of the world; He *is* the Light of the World. He does not merely know all of the truth; He *is* the truth.

Thus, it follows that truth (for example) is not an abstract concept discovered by some primitive philosopher upon the dawning of civilization. Rather, truth is a Person. Similarly, life is not merely a biological phenomenon, but instead a Person. Pontius Pilate did not grasp this concept when he asked Jesus, "What is truth" (John 18:38)? The real question is not "what," but "who."

The full extent of the revelation of God given to us by His names is quite profound. This brief study can only hint at the depths of that revelation. The old shepherd named Moses who stood on a mountain in the wilderness in the presence of God probably never suspected the full scope of the revelation that would be set in motion by his simple request to know God by name.

CHAPTER 19
Decoding the Birth Pangs of Israel

The longest pregnancy in recorded history lasted about four thousand years. It began with God's promise to Adam and Eve that He would send a Savior, and it ended with the birth of Jesus in the town of Bethlehem. Though we have examined this promise before, it bears repeating. The promise was actually spoken to the Serpent, and it foretold Satan's doom: "And I will put enmity between you and the woman, and between your offspring and hers; he will crush your head, and you will strike his heel" (Genesis 3:15).

Thus, the Lord announced that a male descendant of Eve would crush the head of the Serpent, though the male descendant would have His heel injured in the process. The remainder of the Old Testament is largely the account of how God dealt with the human race so as to prepare the way for this promised male descendant who would defeat the Devil and atone for Adam and Eve's transgression.

There is a passage in the book of Revelation that reinforces this view of human history. The passage, Revelation 12:1-6, starts out by describing a supernatural vision given to John on the island of Patmos: "A great sign appeared in heaven: a woman clothed with the sun, with the moon under her feet and a crown of twelve stars on her head" (Revelation 12:1).

It is necessary to determine the identity of the woman before we proceed any further with this passage; otherwise, the passage will appear to be meaningless. The woman can be readily identified, but we must go all the way back to the book of Genesis and look at one of Joseph's dreams in order to do so. You may recall that Joseph had a series of dreams that angered his brothers and turned them against him. These dreams predicted that his brothers would one day bow down before him. He described one particular dream in this way: "'Listen,' he said, 'I had another dream, and this time the sun and moon and eleven stars were bowing down to me'" (Genesis 37:9). The imagery here is very similar to the imagery found in the Revelation passage. Joseph's father, Jacob, being a gifted man of God in his own right, provided the interpretation to this dream: "When he told his father as well as his brothers, his father rebuked him and said, 'What is this dream you had? Will your mother and I and your brothers actually come and bow down to the ground before you'" (Genesis 37:10)?

Thus, we see the meaning of the symbols: The sun represented Jacob, who was the ancestor of all the Israelites. The moon represented Jacob's wife, and the eleven stars represented the eleven brothers of Joseph.

In the Revelation passage, the twelfth star must have represented Joseph himself. Thus, the woman is associated with Jacob and his wife, and she is wearing a crown that represents the twelve tribes of Israel. This woman can only represent the nation of Israel itself. This interpretation is supported by the fact that Israel is also symbolized as a woman in other Scripture passages.

Continuing with the Revelation account, John proceeded to provide additional details about the woman who represented Israel: "She was pregnant and cried out in pain as she was about to give birth" (Revelation 12:2).

It is clear from the writings of the prophet Isaiah that the One to whom Israel was to give birth was the Messiah who was to bring salvation to the earth. Of course, this birth was still some seven hundred years away during Isaiah's time, so Israel was still in the middle of her birth pangs, as indicated by the following passage:

> As a pregnant woman about to give birth writhes and cries out in her pain, so were we in your presence, Lord. We were with child, we writhed in labor, but we gave birth to wind. We have not brought salvation to the earth and the people of the world have not come to life. (Isaiah 26:17–18)

The Revelation account then describes the forces arrayed against this birth: "Then another sign appeared in heaven: an enormous red dragon with seven heads and ten horns and seven crowns on its heads. Its tail swept a third of the stars out of the sky and flung them to the earth" (Revelation 12:3–4).

The identity of the dragon and the stars under its control is clear from a subsequent passage, Revelation 12:9: "The great dragon was hurled down—that ancient serpent called the devil, or Satan, who leads the whole world astray. He was hurled to the earth, and his angels with him."

The next passage we will examine describes graphically the Devil's active opposition to Israel and her promised Messiah: "The dragon stood in front of the woman who was about to give birth, so that it might devour her child the moment he was born" (Revelation 12:4).

King Herod was the primary tool used by the Devil in this attempt to destroy the Christ child in His cradle. Herod murdered all of the male babies in the vicinity of Bethlehem in an attempt to kill the future King. But by this time, Jesus was safely in Egypt since His earthly father had been warned by an angel to take Him there ahead of Herod's murderous rampage.

As we look at human history leading up to the birth of Jesus, we see that the Devil tried to thwart the arrival of God's promised Messiah at every turn, not just when Jesus was born. In fact, we can see that the overriding thought in Satan's mind and the intent of Satan's heart was to *stop the offspring of the woman* by any means possible. Since the Messiah was first identified only as a male descendant of Eve, the Devil first tried to corrupt the whole human race in an attempt to block the offspring of the woman. The human race did become almost completely corrupted, but the Devil's plan failed when God brought forth a flood to wipe out the corruption while preserving Noah and his family.

After several more generations, the Devil mounted another attack. He almost succeeded in bringing about a single world government under his control, centered at the Tower of Babel. But the Lord confused the languages (and possibly also the ethnic traits) of the people and scattered them over the face of the earth. This action created barriers that made it virtually impossible to unite the entire world under one government again for thousands of years. This allowed Jesus to survive Herod's campaign of infanticide by ensuring that there would be a foreign haven to which He and His parents could flee for refuge.

Having made a world of many cultures, languages, and ethnic groups, the Lord then selected one of them as His special vehicle to bring forth a Messiah for the whole world. That God intended for this Messiah to bring salvation to the whole world there can be no doubt, for God told Abraham that *"all peoples on earth will be blessed through you"* (Genesis 12:3; emphasis mine).

When God narrowed down the bloodline of the Messiah to a single ethnic group (the Israelites), the Devil responded by directing his fury and cunning against this chosen group. He first had them enslaved in Egypt, and then he caused several competing groups to move into and occupy the land promised to them as Abraham's descendants. After the Lord brought His people out of Egypt and into the Promised Land, many people from these groups remained as "barbs in [the Israelites'] eyes and thorns in [their] sides" (Numbers 33:55) for the duration of Israel's history.

After several more centuries, the Lord further narrowed down the bloodline of the promised Messiah by identifying Him as a descendant of King David. The Devil responded by attacking the royal line, bringing temptation and corruption to the kings of Israel and Judah and inspiring attempts on the lives of some of the royal heirs. The people of Israel and of Judah were subject to exile as a result. They were finally brought under foreign domination, first by the Greeks and then by the Romans. Nevertheless, God's plan was still in operation. So when the time was right, God brought forth a Son from Mary's womb conceived by the Holy Spirit.

At last, the specific male "offspring" promised in Genesis 3:15 had arrived. The Devil proceeded to direct his full fury and guile against Jesus personally. This resulted in Herod's attempt on the child's life mentioned earlier. It also resulted in the Devil's attempt to recruit Jesus for his own cause when he tempted Jesus in the wilderness. When that attempt failed, the Devil tried to kill Jesus by hatching plots against Him and by provoking mobs into attacking Him.

As Jesus gave up His life on the cross, it must have seemed to the Devil that he had finally defeated the Messiah and thwarted God's plan to save the world. But the Devil, in his blind fury, failed to realize he had played right into God's hands and had brought about the perfect sacrifice through which Jesus was able to atone for the sins of the world. After this atoning sacrifice was complete, God raised Jesus from the dead and brought Him up to heaven. Next began the preparations for Jesus to return to earth in great glory to rule the world. Thus, the Revelation passage concerning the nation of Israel concludes by telling of the birth of Jesus and of His ascension into heaven: "She gave birth to a son, a male child, who will rule all the nations with an iron scepter. And her child was snatched up to God and to his throne" (Revelation 12:5).

The next several verses describe the great tribulation, an event that has not yet come to pass. This will represent one more desperate attempt by Satan to thwart God's plan. This attempt, like the others that came before it, will also fail. Jesus will return to earth to set up His kingdom and to bring about eternal defeat and punishment for Satan.

Thus, Satan's doom is assured. Why, then, does he continue to resist? Why does he continue his attempts to deceive, steal, kill, and destroy? Perhaps it is as Hal Lindsay once suggested: Maybe the Devil's master plan now is to prevent as many people as possible from coming to salvation through Jesus Christ. If enough people stay lost, the Devil may reason, then God may have to compromise His principles by making a deal with those who refused to accept Christ as Savior. If God will make a deal with these people in order to avoid condemning them, then perhaps God will have to offer the Devil a deal as well. If this is in fact the Devil's reasoning (it is only a theory, but an interesting one), it is fatally flawed, because our God is a righteous God who will not compromise with evil.

If the Devil cannot stop someone from coming to faith in Jesus Christ, his next step is either to keep them ignorant of the authority they have or to tempt them to commit sins and then demoralize and paralyze them by reminding them of those sins and heaping condemnation on them. That's why, as Christians, if we focus primarily on our sins instead of God's love and forgiveness, we play into the Devil's hands and render ourselves ineffective at the job of spreading God's kingdom throughout the earth.

On the other hand, if we remember who we are, and *whose* we are, then we, the church, are Satan's worst nightmare: a group of blood-bought believers who are filled with the Holy Spirit and who have the authority to do the same works that Christ did, and even greater, in order to advance the kingdom of God over the earth and destroy the works of Satan.

CHAPTER 20
The Holographic Testament

Is God still speaking to us today and revealing things to us in modern times? Since God spoke to our ancestors "at many times and in various ways" (Hebrews 1:1), progressively revealing more and more about Himself, it only makes sense that He is still revealing truths to us today, even though the Scriptures, the yardstick by which we must evaluate new information, are settled and finished.

I've been interested in science my whole life. One of the things that has always intrigued me is the hologram, which is like a three-dimensional photo. Perhaps you have seen one of these on a credit card or on some other object designed to be hard to counterfeit. Here is a brief excerpt about holograms from *Encyclopedia.com*:

> Although a hologram is a visual image of a physical object, it is quite different from a photograph. For instance, when an object is photographed, each portion of the photo contains an image of the corresponding portion of the original object. Each section of a hologram, however, contains a complete image of the original object, viewed from a vantage point that corresponds to the section's position on the hologram. Thus, if the ... hologram is

broken, each piece will still be able to project the entire image, albeit from a different point of view. Using a piece from near the top of the holographic plate will produce an image as seen from above, while using a piece from near the bottom of the plate will create the impression of looking upward toward the object.

A hologram must be illuminated by a laser to take full advantage of its 3-D image attributes and to allow the entire object to be seen in any one of its pieces.

If the New Testament can be likened to an optical photograph of Jesus Christ, then the Old Testament would be like a *hologram* of Christ and His redemptive work in our lives. When the Old Testament is viewed in the correct light, its pages come alive with types, images, and prophecies of Christ, each one representing Christ from a certain point of view and emphasizing some aspect of His life and work. This is true whether we look at the Old Testament as a whole (the point of view of chapter 19) or at specific passages, down to small fragments. Through the modern invention of the hologram, God demonstrates today to scientists who have eyes to see that the Old Testament has been modeling a hologram all along.

Some additional thoughts relating to modern times are in order. Since many of the characters, events, and symbols of Old Testament times point forward to Jesus Christ, it is only natural to ask whether any of the characters, events, and symbols of modern times point backward to Christ. The answer is undoubtedly yes. There could be many reasons why this is so. Both conscious and unconscious factors may result in references to Christ in contemporary culture. The unconscious references are, if anything, more notable and significant than the conscious references because these references are the result of the Holy Spirit operating today.

Decoding Bible Messages

It may come as a surprise to those who are not familiar with the study of types, but many fictional folk heroes in books, movies, television, and elsewhere are symbolic portrayals of Christ in many of their attributes. These attributes could include any of a number of characteristics that set these characters apart from the rest of humanity, including unusual skills or abilities, supernatural powers, high intelligence, extraordinary physical strength, etc.

This is not to say that the authors, scriptwriters, and producers deliberately instilled Christlike characteristics into their fictional characters. On the contrary, this is probably quite inadvertent in most cases. Nevertheless, it is certain that this is an indication embedded in our culture of our need for a Savior, however unconscious this need may be. The popularity of some of these characters is therefore indicative of the Christ-shaped void in people's hearts and of our culture's attempts to fill that hole.

As an illustration, consider *E.T., the Extra-Terrestrial*. The character E.T. was not of this world. He died and was raised from the dead. He could heal by touching people. He could perform supernatural feats. He had great appeal to children, as he was gentle and loving, but he was not accepted by adults. He was kept hidden. Finally, he ascended into the heavens. Before that, he promised to maintain a link somehow with the boy's mind after he left (symbolizing the indwelling of the Holy Spirit?).

Another example is Mr. Spock of *Star Trek* fame, particularly in *Star Trek II: The Wrath of Khan* and *Star Trek III: The Search for Spock*. Spock was an individual of extraordinary intelligence and ability, as illustrated, for example, by the "Vulcan mind meld," whereby he could discern the thoughts of other people. His mother was an earthling, but his father was not of this world. In *Star Trek II*, he sacrificed himself and died to save the *Enterprise* and its crew. Just before he died, he called Captain Kirk his friend. In the next sequel,

Star Trek III, he was resurrected. The movies revolve around an endeavor called the Genesis Project.

Superman, of course, is another illustration of this tendency in our culture to instill Christlike attributes in our heroes. Superman was not of this world, had superhuman powers, performed extraordinary acts, etc.

Neo of *The Matrix* trilogy is yet another example.

Numerous other examples could be cited. Suffice it to say that the popularity of these characters attests to the crying need in people's hearts for the presence of Christ.

We need look no farther than Jesus Christ Himself for the realization of our deepest longings. We have in Jesus Christ the fulfillment of all of the hopes, dreams, ambitions, and aspirations that God has built into the human heart and mind. All of the types we have examined in this book point to Jesus, as all compasses point to the North Pole. No one in history except Jesus had a series of encoded biographies written about him between five hundred and two thousand years before his birth. But the Old Testament is just such a document for Jesus, as this book has shown.

It is my hope that through this book, Christian readers may come to a more firmly rooted and gladly held conviction that Jesus Christ is Lord, and that skeptical, inquiring readers may obtain enough new evidence to trigger that final leap of faith required for Jesus to come alive in their hearts.

BIBLIOGRAPHY

Beasley, Bob. *101 Portraits of Jesus in the Hebrew Scriptures*. Hendersonville, NC: Living Stone Books, 2008.

Buksbazen, Victor. *The Gospel in the Feasts of Israel*. Fort Washington, PA: Christian Literature Crusade, 1954.

Bullinger, E. W. *How to Enjoy the Bible*. London: Samuel Bagster & Sons Ltd., reprinted 1980.

Habershon, Ada R. *The Study of the Types*. Grand Rapids, MI: Kregel Publications, reprinted 1981.

———. *Hidden Pictures in the Old Testament*. Grand Rapids, MI: Kregel Publications, reprinted 1982.

"Hologram," in "How Products Are Made." 1998. *Encyclopedia.com*. (May 26, 2015) http://www.encyclopedia.com/doc/1G2-2896700054.html.

Jukes, Andrew. *Types in Genesis*. Grand Rapids, MI: Kregel Publications, reprinted 1981.

Norten, Michael. *Unlocking the Secrets of the Feasts*. Nashville: WestBow Press, 2015.

Pillai, Bishop K. C. *Light through an Eastern Window*. New York: Robert Speller and Sons, 1963.

Rice, John R. *Christ in the Old Testament*. Murfreesboro: Sword of the Lord Publishers, 1969.

White, John Wesley. *The Man from Krypton: The Gospel According to Superman*. Minneapolis: Bethany Fellowship, Inc., 1978.

THE AUTHOR

John A. Mapp Jr. lives with his wife, Kathy, in the upstate of South Carolina. He is a retired senior systems analyst who worked for a large defense contractor. A native of Virginia, he spent the majority of his life in central Florida. John is a graduate of Hampden-Sydney College in Virginia, where he majored in physics. He received a master's degree in business administration from the Mason School of Business at the College of William and Mary. He and Kathy have a grown son, a grown daughter, and a young grandson.

John is an autodidact, being able to research and master new subjects with little or no formal instruction. While working in Florida, John led small groups for single and young adult members of his church, and also taught various classes. After John married Kathy in 1988, the couple homeschooled their children for most of their school years. John and Kathy subsequently had a ministry working with local Mexican immigrant families, which helped John learn enough Spanish to become substantially bilingual. In 2011, John and Kathy were ordained as pastors by House of Praise Ministries, Grove City, Ohio. John's fascination with the subject matter of this book dates from the early 1980s.

Printed in the United States
By Bookmasters